# Primary Geography, Primary History

# Primary Geography, Primary History

**Peter Knight**

**David Fulton Publishers**
London

David Fulton Publishers Ltd
2 Barbon Close, London WC1N 3JX

First published in Great Britain by
David Fulton Publishers 1993

Copyright © Peter Knight

*British Library Cataloguing in Publication Data*

A catalogue record for this book is available from the British Library

ISBN 1-85346-207-1

**Typeset by The Brightside Partnership**
**Printed in Great Britain by BPCC Journals, Exeter**

# Contents

Foreword by Peter Robinson ............................................ vi

Preface ...................................................................... vii

1    A Research Perspective ..................................... 1

2    The Primary School ........................................ 6

3    Teaching.......................................................... 14

4    Children .......................................................... 25

5    The Nature of Geography ................................. 38

6    Primary School Geography .............................. 49

7    The Study of History ....................................... 82

8    History in the Primary School ......................... 89

9    Arguments about Integration ........................... 102

10   Re-integrating the Primary
      Curriculum...................................................... 126

11   Professional Development for
      Primary Humanities......................................... 141

12   Lurching after Chimeras? ................................. 153

      References ....................................................... 161

      Index .............................................................. 176

# Foreword

It used to be difficult to achieve consensus in the teaching profession, but at the present time several propositions might be found which would command universal assent. One is that the time needed to teach the National Curriculum and to fulfil other new and old statutory requirements, greatly exceeds that available in the school year.

Hence, mandatory as geography and history are, their coverage is likely to be squeezed in any primary timetable stretched both by legal demands and by aspirations of schools to appear higher in academic league tables. Peter Knight argues for the educational virtues of geography and history and the opportunities they offer primary teachers. He sets their possibilities in the wider framework of what recent research has shown can help to promote quality in primary education at the level of school and classrooms.

The four chapters about geography and history form the substantive subject core. These remind us of the qualities of the two disciplines and the contexts in which these might be promoted in primary schools. They summarise some weaknesses of earlier practice, comment on recent research and illustrate how current and future practices might take advantage of developments in our knowledge. Two further chapters set out arguments against and for the integration of the teaching of geography and history, and show how re-integration might be achieved and what its educational benefits can be. So much that is good and worthwhile could and can be done, given the single proviso that the demands on schools and their staff do not exceed what is feasible. Peter Knight helps to formulate ways of maximising educational gains for children without further overloading the timetables.

Peter Robinson
Bristol
March 1993

# *Preface*

In English schools history and geography are mandatory subjects, neglected despite their position in the National Curriculum, and under pressure as schools try to find ways of boosting children's publicly reported scores in maths, English and science. In Scotland, New Zealand, Canada, France, Australia and the USA the situation is similar, no matter what name the subjects take, no matter how they are organised.

Yet geography and history *are* part of the primary curriculum and concern is still shown when it is reported that children are geographically illiterate and ignorant of great events in national history.

This book is based on the belief that general research into schools, children and teaching has a great deal to say about effective social studies and humanities teaching (when I use these terms it is geography and history only that I have in mind). This research is a resource frequently ignored by writers who have the school subject to the fore and everything else hidden by their enthusiasm for it.

I also believe that detailed though the English National Curriculum is, it still gives teachers some choice of topics, leaves assessment in the social studies in their hands, requires considerable interpretation (what does it mean to say that most 7 year olds should offer an explanation of why people acted as they did?), prescribes no pedagogy, and, quite simply, that it needs to be implemented by schools, by teachers, through children. Curriculum design, in its most obvious forms, may have been taken over by mandarins who began growing their fingernails at prep school, but curriculum implementation, which transforms plans, is the teachers' preserve.

Inevitably, there is a lot here about teaching techniques, but this is not primarily a book on how to teach geography or history – it is more a book to stimulate thought and professional, autonomous but co-operative action. As a result there are no topic plans for teaching about modern Greece or medieval Benin. Likewise, I have only had the space viii

to deal with issues as they relate to primary education generally, so there are few explicit distinctions made between Juniors and Infants; children with and without special educational needs; or town and country children. You, the reader, will need to ask whether *that* research applies to *these* circumstances. I just hope that I prompt you to ask 'why?' or 'why not?' and to continue to engage in that vigorous professionalism which is necessary if the quintessence of good primary practice, as we have known it, is to survive the twentieth century.

Mrs Angela Milner, of the Open University and Mr Chris Rowley, of this university's Department of Undergraduate Teacher Education, read Chapter 6 in draft, while Chris also read Chapter 8. Dr Anne Edwards, of St Martin's College read Chapter 4. Ms Alison Green, of Ghyllside Primary School, Kendal and Professor Stephen Thornton, of the Teachers' College at Columbia University, have kindly read the whole book in draft. None of them is responsible for my eccentricities and errors. Thanks to them for restraining my excesses!

Peter Knight
Lancaster University

# Chapter 1

# A Research Perspective

## The futility of research

Many teachers have little time for research and feel that the best contribution which researchers could make to improving practice would be to retire and thereby free funds which could be used to hire teachers, buy books and pay for educational visits. Schon (1987) has shown that teachers are not alone in this impatience with research and theories, adding architects, social workers and medical practitioners to the list (see also Argyris *et al*, 1985).

Practitioners often complain that researchers write gobbledegook.

A further source of dissatisfaction is that researchers usually try to comment upon schools, children and classes *in general,* so their reports often lack those specific details which add immediacy and conviction. Even where they include case studies and vignettes, there is no guarantee that the case studies will particularly resemble the context in which the reader works and with which the reader is concerned. Quite simply, research reports are not about the reader's school and an act of imagination is necessary to make them relevant to it.

A more subtle problem is that researchers often identify and give importance to factors which are not immediately apparent in daily practice. The idea that different children have different motivational styles is a powerful one, but the concept of motivational style is not immediately apparent in daily classroom practice. The teacher who reads this research (Rogers, 1990) has still got a lot of thinking to do before her practice is affected.

It is sometimes said that teachers are born not made. Another common claim is that expertise in teaching comes from experience. Both views tend to exclude theories of the sort generated by research.

2

Besides, research findings, it is often said, are no more than expensively garnered common sense.

A fifth complaint is that research is insensitive to practitioners, since it is something done to practitioners, with the result that the 'outsider's arrogance' (McNamara, 1980) leads to the teacher's perspectives being measured and valued according to how far they conform to the researcher's. In this way research is not teacher-friendly.

A variant of this is that research and researchers threaten the teachers' existing competence, for example by claiming that they fail to match the work to many of their students' achievements (Bennett *et al*, 1984; Desforges and Cockburn, 1987), or by presenting models of good practice which are not easily achieved in busy classrooms (Slavin, 1990). Research can easily be seen as ever critical of practitioners, having a deficit view of the teacher who is urged to change by 'ivory tower' people who are not themselves faced with the daily press of school teaching (Elliott, 1991a).

Also, of course, the questions which researchers want to study are often not the ones which worry teachers. Shaver (1987) pointed out that educationists tend not to study teacher concerns with classroom management and techniques for getting children to learn content more effectively, while teachers rarely plan their curricula in the rational manner favoured by some curriculum theorists.

**False assumptions**

These criticisms will be addressed in two ways: first by contesting some of their assumptions and secondly by arguing that research is a worthwhile activity.

Some research reports are indeed technical, use a technical language and are hard going. The research community is aware of the problem. Shaver introduced *The Handbook of Research on Social Studies Teaching and Learning* saying that, 'I sought clear, direct writing ... I put my editor's pencil to obtuse words and phrases, and to complex, obscure sentences' (1991, p.x) and *School Matters*, one of the most important British research studies of the 1980s is written throughout in jargon free, plain, honest prose.

The idea that research is an expensive way of getting at common sense rests on false ideas about common sense. Which is true – that increasing parental choice of schools will improve or harm educational standards? That children's style of work is the same irrespective of the teacher who they have, or that it changes according to the teacher? That schools make a substantial difference to children's life chances, or that non-educational factors essentially determine those chances? In each case either answer could claim to be 'common sense'; research can make it clearer which really is 'common sense', showing that 'common sense' is often neither sensible nor common.

The complaint that research findings are general and insensitive to the special situation of each reader is understandable but odd, nevertheless. Three assumptions seem to be involved: that the particular is of interest, the general is not; that research provides solutions; and that teachers are educational operatives, not professionals. Now, if teachers were piece workers, paid only to follow well-defined routines, then there would be little need for them to compare their situations and practices with those in the wider world, because authority would tell them what to do. As professionals, however much their autonomy may have been trimmed in recent years, teachers need to enquire about education *in general* in order to be able to choose well and to account for those choices. In one sense, then, it is disappointing that research does not and cannot provide solutions: it is not prescriptive, but permissive (Smith, 1986) – that is to say it does not produce codes for practitioners to follow but it does produce healthy food for thought.

This will disappoint those who assume that research should produce prescriptions in the same way as technological research produces a better motor car engine, a stronger glue or a bubblier washing-up liquid. That is impossible in social research. As a consequence, research demands a truly professional audience to appreciate it, winnow it and work it into forms usable in particular contexts. If research produced prescriptions, then it would imply that schools should be filled with robo-teachers, the operatives of an educational mill. Research goes hand-in-hand with teacher professionalism.

## The meanings of educational research

If criticisms of educational research are often founded on naive assumptions, they are sustained by ignorance of its diversity.

To many people research is a 'white coat' activity involving large-scale surveys of isolated aspects of the complex job, often done in ignorance of all those factors which mean that real life is essentially different from the statistical abstractions of the researcher's ordered models.

We can better see relevance of this classical research if we recall that teaching is more than what happens in the classroom, although it is *about* what happens in the classroom. Apart from the interactive (in the classroom) phase, there is also the planning (or pre-active) stage and the evaluation (or post-active) stage. It is at these points that research is most potent, as an aid to thinking well about the act of teaching.

A consequence is that the impact of research is concealed because there is a gap between our thinking and our practices, between 'espoused logic' and 'logic-in-use' (Schon, 1987) or between 'propositional' and 'procedural' thinking (Argyris *et al*, 1985). Procedural thinking and logic-in-use are terms referring to that on-the-run thought which shapes our actions as we teach. This sort of thought is shaped by all the exigencies of the daily bustle of practice, by the practitioner's need to react swiftly to circumstances and to cope. Whatever our thinking, practice – and the routines which we have burnt into it – has a life of its own, although it is not a life which cannot be influenced by planning. However, the result is that classical research makes an impact on practice only at one remove, by influencing thinking.

But is this a sufficient definition of research? My preferred definition is that it is systematic enquiry. The enquiries may be into any topic or problem, on any scale, using any fit methods, in any place. And they may be conducted by any person. That definition embraces the 'white coat' research but it also includes 'action research', a concept which owes much to the insights of Professor Stenhouse (Stenhouse, 1975; Walker, 1985; Elliott, 1991a). It is a democratic view in which every teacher has the potential to be her own researcher – indeed, the strong version of this claim says that every teacher needs to be a researcher into her own practice, and the national curricula in the UK rather encourage such a view, with their emphasis on the teacher collecting and then using assessment data formatively in order to improve teaching and learning. It is an integration of systematic enquiry, reflection, action, assessment and evaluation. In the words of Elliott (1991b, p.21),

> A fundamental principle of action research is that it begins with the teacher's own understanding of the practical problems that they face in the classroom with kids. It doesn't start off with a theoretical problem, it starts with a practical problem. It's concerned with understanding and exploring that problem and trying to find ways of resolving that particular problem ... It's about working with this group of kids, in this classroom ... and trying to clarify and reflect ... in a way that helps you to understand it.

This book is based upon two beliefs: that being research literate is better than being research illiterate, bound to the common round of the juggernaut of present practice; and that teaching is a profession, carrying with it the demand for the constant appraisal and re-imagination of what has been done and of what might be done.

The message is that primary geography and history must be the subjects of practical enquiry and that it will be useful if those enquiries are informed by what others have concluded from their own research studies, large and small. And because primary humanities cannot be detached from its contexts – especially the school, the child and the classroom – it is to those that we turn.

# Chapter 2

# The Primary School

## The significance of the school

The growth of research into effective and ineffective schools over the past 15 years represents a change in research ideology, since formerly teachers, children and the curriculum were the main objects of study. Those studies need to be supplemented by insight into the school as an organisation, since what the individual does is done in that organisational context, and is strengthened or weakened by that context. Systems analysts refer to the notion of 'emergence' to refer to the way that a complete system may be bigger or different from the sum of its parts (Checkland, 1981), which is to say that we cannot study effective primary schooling simply by adding together our knowledge of effective curriculum, learning and teaching.

This can be seen in inspection reports published by HMI (the English government school inspectors). They have often remarked on fine work done in some subjects by individual teachers, but have also noted that uneven practice within the individual school has meant that such good work has existed in isolation, so the children's learning has been fragmented, lacking continuity, coherence and progression. This has been true of all curriculum subjects but the social studies, which have a lesser status than maths or English, have been particularly characterised by these discontinuities of practice, both in the USA and in England (Thornton, 1988; DES, 1989a; Thornton and Wenger, 1990). This is a consequence of *school* policies which have valued teacher autonomy above teacher collaboration and consistency. Remedies are school-level remedies. In England this has been partly recognised through the development of 'curriculum co-ordinators', classroom teachers who are semi-specialists in a subject or area and whose job includes the co-ordination of the teaching of a subject throughout the school. However, it cannot be said that the system has solved the school-level problems in 'basic' subjects such as maths, science and English, let alone in the 'frills' (Campbell, 1990).

But the state requires there to be curriculum continuity, consistency and progression and vigorously ensures that its provisions are respected. Is there, then, any significant autonomy left to the individual school? It is helpful to borrow Orton and Weick's analysis (1990), which would show schools to be a part of a loosely coupled system in which they have some freedom of action, although that freedom is somewhat constrained. Moreover, the work of Fullan (1991) on curriculum innovation strongly argues that all innovations become transformed in their implementation as circumstances press on what is perceived to be possible and as individuals work out their own meanings of the innovation. Actually delivering the curriculum – teaching it – further transforms it. Besides, even in England, which now has one of the more tightly coupled education systems, the Secretary of State for Education has disclaimed any intention of dictating teaching methods (DES, 1991a), leaving schools to make their own policies in this crucial area. In short, schools have great scope to be good, bad or indifferent.

The effectiveness of attempts to implement a geography or history curriculum is related to the sort of place a school is – whether the teachers are keen and skilled, whether the school runs smoothly on the basis of shared norms, or whether survival is the name of the game (for children or teachers?); whether information about children's achievements is used, not just collected and stored; whether parents work with the school, or are suspicious or indifferent; whether equal opportunities (for teachers and children?) manifest themselves daily; and in a myriad of other ways, the sort of place a school is affects how any curriculum is going to turn out – subtly, perhaps, but certainly too. In other words schools are places which create their own cultures and, as we shall see, the sort of culture which grows up in a school has a great deal to do with how effective that school is. Rosenholtz (1991) said the influence of the school was so great that teachers' attitudes, their behaviours and their ways of thinking were determined not so much by their own biographies but by the workplace, their school.

Goodlad summarised the position succinctly, *'Schools* differ; *schooling* is everywhere much the same' (1984, p.264). It is to those differences that we now turn.

### Research on effective schools – some limits to knowledge

Surprisingly, there is disagreement about what effective schools are effective at. The liberal hope that schools might redress class inequalities has not been fulfilled, despite many attempts to support working-class participation in education (Jencks *et al*, 1972; Wilson and Corcoran, 1988). There is, however, plenty of evidence that children's education *is* affected by the school they attend and studies have shown a wide variation in the performance of children of similar achievements and from similar backgrounds who attend more or less effective schools (Goodlad, 1984; Mortimore *et al*, 1988; Smith and Tomlinson, 1989; Rosenholtz, 1991).

Since children of widely differing abilities attend different schools, with some schools attracting more able learners whereas children with less propitious characteristics are grouped in other schools, it is not surprising to find that different schools appear to have different levels of effectiveness, as measured by children's *achievement*. Recognising this, researchers have concentrated on children's *progress*, that is, on the educational 'value' which has been added through their time at school. In this way we can imagine a school whose students get high grades but which is an ineffective school because the children joined the school with a high level of achievement and added little to it during their time there. Conversely, a school might be particularly effective despite children leaving it with low achievement scores, since those scores represented a substantial advance on what they could do when entering the school.

This raises the issue of what do we mean when we say that children have made good progress in a school – progress in what? 'Conventional measures of academic achievement may be weak and inadequate indicators of the quality of our schools' (Rosenholtz, 1991, p.213). Some researchers (Mortimore *et al*, 1988; Smith and Tomlinson, 1989) have said that academic progress and good behaviour are associated, so a school which is effective in one tends to be effective in the other. This is a deeply optimistic message, as is the claim that effective schools benefit *all* children, rather than only those who are white, male and clever, for example. However, these claims are disputed.

Critics of the effective school literature have also pointed to:

● methodological problems: (i) the lack of long-term studies; (ii) the reliance on data about children's achievements only in the basic skills; (iii) small sample sizes; (iv) loose and varying definitions of the key variables; and (v) the way that schools at the extremes– the very good and the very bad – can skew the overall picture, implying that school effects are greater than they actually are for most schools.

● a neglect of (i) variation *within* schools: we often make assumptions that a school is a homogenous place, although there is evidence that schools typically harbour a range of teacher attitudes, positions and practices (Rosenholtz, 1991); (ii) variation in school effectiveness over time – research is usually in the form of a snapshot of schools at a point in time: longitudinal studies which show schools becoming better, getting worse or staying the same, are expensive to mount, tricky to negotiate, few in number and immensely valuable.

● the difficulty of using the research findings in order to improve schools. The research identifies factors which go with successful schools. What we don't know is whether these factors are things which caused a school to be successful or which are the *result* of its success. Put another way, it might be that anyone could take over as the headteacher of an effective school and appear to be a good leader. Do great leaders make effective schools, or do effective schools make leaders look great?

● the way that this research could lead to a new orthodoxy about what schools should be like. Two undesirable consequences could follow: the erosion of innovation and risk-taking; and a drive towards uniformity at a time when it is still not clear how far schools need to differ if they are to be effective with different groups of parents and students.

On the basis of these points it might be assumed that the concept of an effective school was crumbling away. The difficulties with research methodologies should not obscure the regular reports from independent research projects which show that schools do make a difference. However, the concept of there being one type of effectiveness is not sustainable and must be replaced by a multi-faceted view of effectiveness, which recognises the different senses in which schools might claim success. Simple formulae for school evaluation and improvement should not be the outcome of this research, which is consistent with the view of educational research as a way of supplying concepts that will help people to think hard.

That said, it is appropriate to assert again that good primary geography and history work go with effective schools. Good humanities work builds on last year's good work and leads to next year's. If a school-wide approach is not in evidence, then this year's good work must start from scratch and lead nowhere. In that spirit we can consider some of the findings about effective schools.

## Effective primary schools

Purkey and Smith published 'Effective Schools: A Review' in 1983. They listed thirteen factors associated with effective schools, four of which they called 'process dimensions', that is characteristics of the culture of the school, and nine 'organisational-structural' dimensions.

The organisational factors were:

● school-site management;
● instructional leadership;
● staff stability;
● curriculum organisation;
● whole-school staff development;
● parental involvement;
● school-wide recognition of academic achievement;
● maximised learning time;
● support from the district (or the Local Education Authority (LEA) in England).

Studies of successful *secondary* schools have provided some evidence supporting this list. However, there are problems in deciding exactly what these terms mean – what level and type of parental involvement is associated with successful schools? Is it the same in all successful schools, irrespective of their catchment areas and histories? Or, concerning instructional leadership, Wilson and Corcoran (1988, p.13) remark,

> Everyone agrees that visible and active instructional leadership is important to school success, but there is no clear pattern to guide principals or others in potential leadership roles ... leadership functions are carried out differently and successful styles vary with context.

They might also have added that the sex of the leader also seems to be relevant, with men and women tending to have different leadership styles (Ferrario, 1991).

There is greater agreement about the process dimensions, which are:

- collaborative planning and collegial relationships;
- a sense of community;
- clear goals and high expectations;
- 'An environment which is quiet, safe and non-distracting promotes learning'.

There is agreement about these points in the secondary school research, although, again, there are obvious problems of measurement and definition: does not collegiality necessitate a sense of community, and if so, what is the distinction between the concepts (A. Hargreaves, 1992)?

Mortimore and colleagues (1988) examined 50 London junior schools catering for 7–11 year olds over a period of four years. They insisted that successful schools were those in which children made the greatest *progress:* children's achievements might be high or low, as was noted above, largely because of background factors such as socio-economic status.

Their list of the twelve correlates of effective junior schools embraces Purkey and Smith's process dimensions, although they used somewhat different terminology, describing key factors as 'intellectually challenging teaching', 'positive climate', 'work-centred environment', 'the involvement of teachers', and 'consistency amongst teachers'.

Their term 'structured sessions' is similar to Purkey and Smith's organisational dimension of 'maximised learning time', and their terms 'parental involvement and support', and 'purposeful leadership of the staff by the headteacher', also fit into this set of organisational dimensions.

Four of Mortimore's points are distinctive: the involvement of the deputy head; limited focus within sessions; maximum communication between teachers and pupils; and record keeping. The first of these is just a development of the idea that successful schools are well led. The other three refer to the way teaching and learning proceed, and will be discussed in more detail in the next chapter. It is worth emphasising that this study avers that teaching and learning methods are a whole-school affair, not a matter for the individual teacher alone.

Rosenholtz (1991) surveyed 1,213 Tennessee elementary school teachers and interviewed 74 of them from 23 schools in eight districts. Her findings are not directly comparable with the works discussed above since she was interested in the interplay between teachers and their schools, and she grouped and re-grouped teachers for analytical purposes in ways which make it impossible to say how many of the schools which were characterised by shared school goals also provided plentiful learning opportunities for teachers and encouraged them to feel that they could influence children's learning. Yet, it is clear that a number of themes which have already been raised also characterised the better Tennessee schools. These include collegiality; clarity about goals which have been collectively discussed and which are then woven into the system of evaluation; discussion of learning, which is supported by principals who emphasise and are good at problem-working and who are not 'a scolding presence' (p.56); an atmosphere of continued professional learning through professional engagement with the distinctly non-routine business of promoting children's learning; and a belief that students are not innately bound to mediocrity, but that they – and their teachers – can learn and achieve.

As we have noticed, there is a shortage of spells to make schools effective, a shortage which may be becoming even more severe if Rosenholtz is right in arguing that,

> if they [schools] allow too little freedom for their faculty, they are likely to produce oppressed, alienated, and uncaring teachers who are equally unproductive ... ill-conceived bureaucratic control exercised over teachers ... weakened their effectiveness and fouled their commitment (p.161).

Her remark was pointed because the state of Tennessee was bent upon controlling teachers more tightly, with what Rosenholtz saw as detrimental effects. What happened there has been repeated and extended in England and seems to tantalise other states too with its fundamentalist allure. Research, however, argues that teachers are motivated by the psychic rewards of teaching and, 'the less teachers' workplace alienation, the more students achieve' (p.162). Increased control could be counterproductive for,

> teachers' terminal boredom, the loss of their original meaning, their overwhelming sense of unappreciation, and their lack of professional empowerment costs stuck schools dearly: they usurp teachers' capacity to dream (p.165).

This directs us to a key feature of effective schools, their culture. Nias *et al* (1992) have shown the importance of shared values in whole-school curriculum development,

We noted five [values]: learning; interdependence and teamwork; the open expression of professional differences; mutual consideration and support; willingness to compromise. The last four of these are also characteristic of a 'culture of collaboration' (p.236).

All writers on school effectiveness stress that leadership is the key, that it is the head who has a considerable influence on the culture of the school, and hence upon its practices and policies. Southworth (1990) has offered a list of sixteen characteristics of the effective primary headteacher, one of which is that s/he, 'nurtures and maintains a school culture which is inclusive of the school's staff and which facilitates professional and social collaboration', and another is that s/he, 'is considerate towards staff ... takes an interest in staff as people' (p.14). This is not only true of education. In their study of effective big business Peters and Waterman (1982, p.26) argued that, 'it appears that the real role of the chief executive is to manage the *values* of the organisation' and that, 'it is *attention to employees*, not work conditions per se, that has the dominant impact on productivity' (p.6). In Rosenholtz' words (1991, p.56) effective school principals are not, 'a scolding presence, a direct threat to [teachers'] sense of self worth', rather they, 'seem to empower and join with teachers in school improvement, thereby enhancing their professional confidence' (p.64).

To flourish the humanities need to be nested in effective schools. Humane leadership is one characteristic of such schools, shared values another and, as the lists provided by Mortimore and by Purkey and Smith show, certain classroom practices are a third characteristic. Rosenholtz summarised the general message by saying that 'the successful school is a non-routine technical culture where teaching professionals are asked to make reflection and its requisites the master of action and its requisites' (1991, p.214), which is a view that is remarkably close to the notion of the teacher as an action researcher in her own classroom which was outlined in the previous chapter. Keeping in mind the idea that an action research disposition may be a sign of an effective school, we now turn to the classroom to probe the nature of effective teaching.

*Chapter 3*

# Teaching

Myths about teaching have a fascination for the English press, which appears to believe that trendy, child-centred methods dominate primary schools and are to blame for supposedly lamentable educational standards. Research shows that little could be further from the truth.

## Research findings

The work of Galton and associates (1989; 1990), first through the ORACLE project and then in the PRISMS, small schools study, is a major source of information. In the ORACLE study 58 classes were studied in 19 schools, with the students, aged between 8 and 10 at the beginning of the study, being observed for one or two years in primary or middle school and for a further year after transfer to secondary or middle school.

The research was done against the background of the Plowden Report, which had commended child-centred, individualised, flexible and informal teaching methods, and of research which was understood to show that more formal teaching styles were associated with greater pupil progress.

The ORACLE data were analysed to give six groups of teachers, each of whom could be described as having a teaching style. Noting, as Bennett was subsequently to do (1988), that there were considerable variations *within* teaching styles, Galton nevertheless identified differences *between* them as well. 'Individual monitors', who were the closest to informal, Plowden teachers, accounted for just 13 of the sample. Their work was dominated by brief exchanges with individual children. Their main concerns were managerial, particularly through marking children's work to keep them on task. The cognitive level – that is to say the demand made upon children's thinking – of these exchanges was reckoned to be low. Ironically, whereas Plowden saw individualisation as a way of maximising intellectual stimulation, the teachers who worked most through individual contact provided little stimulation. 'Group instructors', comprising seven teachers, worked three times as much with groups of children as did other teachers, even though they only spent some 18 per cent of their time working in this way. Working with groups gave them more time to spend in questioning, and they were able to make more relatively high level factual statements than the 'individual monitors', to ask more 'open questions', and to give more feedback to children. They did, however, incline to instruct rather than to emphasise problem solving.

A third group comprised nine 'class enquirers'. Thirty-one per cent of observations showed them working with the whole class. They asked more challenging questions and made more statements of ideas than other teachers. They were seen as generally emphasising problem solving, fostering a positive classroom climate and using a lot of praise. Although their work had overtones of direct instruction, Galton emphasised that this was not a regime in which children were straitjacketed and in a later work (Galton, 1989) he noted that direct instruction had plenty of advantages, although he preferred a more flexible approach, close to that adopted by the fourth group, described as 'infrequent changers', since their strategies were seen to change to take account of developments within their classes. They were adept at open and closed questioning, avoided a lot of dead time and were good at giving children feedback on their work. There is a case for saying that these teachers were demonstrating reflective thinking, which led them to alter practices in order to keep in pursuit of their educational goals. This type of thinking, reminiscent of an action research orientation, has been identified as a highly desirable characteristic in teachers (Pollard and Tann, 1987).

Inevitably the question arises of which was the most effective of these groups. We must recognise, first, that the degree of overlap among these groups – 'if "progressivism" is defined in terms of freedom, activity and a curriculum based on the needs and interests of the children, then such practices were characteristic of some teachers in each of the ORACLE styles' (Galton, 1989, p.52). That said, then using data on reading, language and mathematics, the infrequent changers and the class enquirers appeared to be the most effective.

Does it then follow that certain ways of working are more effective?

Certainly there are such claims. Rosenshine (1983) argued that teachers are most effective when they:

- structure the learning;
- proceed briskly in small steps;
- give detailed and relevant instructions and explanations;
- provide plenty of examples;
- ask large numbers of questions and provide overt, active practice;
- provide feedback and corrections;
- divide seatwork assignments into smaller assignments;
- provide continued practice (recapitulation).

Reviewing the literature Anderson and Burns (1989) concurred, saying that, 'while lecture recitation and seatwork predominate in classrooms, there is little if any evidence that changes in format would result in higher levels of student achievement' (p.352). Yet, whatever strength direct instruction may have as a way of teaching fixed propositions and routines, it is patently unsuited to many types of learning, especially those to do with application, problem-working, evaluating and creating. Galton (1989) criticised it for not giving children enough control over how they learned and for eroding the challenge of learning. Peterson (1979) concluded that less formal methods of teaching were appropriate to some areas of learning, and that they were effective in those contexts.

However, 'as long as there is one teacher and a large number of children, then the time-honoured 'chalk and talk' method of teaching might actually be the best' (Thomas, 1992, p.66). Discussing individualised teaching, Thomas argued that the case for it was philosophically compelling but, as Goodlad had observed of American schools 'each student works and achieves alone within a group setting' (1984, p.123) and the work was typically not matched to the individual's learning needs. In the words of researchers into 4 year olds in school,

> The problems of matching, monitoring and diagnosing are all intertwined, and all occur as a consequence of teachers' persistence in attempts to implement and maintain a philosophy of individualisation. It is this which is at the core of the problem. And the reason is simple. Individualisation is impossible (Bennett and Kell, 1989, p.85).

Not only are there problems in seeing whole-class or individualised teaching as hallmarks of effective teaching, there are problems too with group-work. This has attractions as a compromise between the other two methods, avoiding the pitfalls of both and achieving the benefits of each. Yet, Bennett and colleagues (1984), and Galton (1989) reported failure in their attempts to turn group-work from being an organisational device into a learning device. Slavin (1990) reported success but only by adopting some rather complicated classroom practices, which are discussed in the next chapter.

No one method of teaching has proved to be invariably superior to others. The most we can say is that each of these approaches should be used when appropriate, which is hardly a helpful formula to apply to the identification of good teaching.

**Teaching as exposure**

The English National Curriculum has rolled together many views of education, so it is not easy to say that it particularly embodies any one conception of effective teaching. However, the emphasis which it places on children mastering a given set of propositional and procedural knowledge means that it is plausible to claim that effective teaching in England now entails ensuring that children are exposed to this range of knowledge *and* ensuring that they know what they have learned.

It follows that one criterion of an effective teacher is that her curriculum *at least* covers what the state has required.

Exposure without awareness will be insufficient. Writing of mathematics, Howson (1991) echoed this as he criticised naive forms of 'discovery learning',

> Activities cannot be allowed to degenerate into time-fillers from which children are expected to learn in a purely random manner ... Understanding develops with use and in considering a curriculum we shall want to see how a pupil is helped to consolidate, revise, reinforce and deepen understanding ... The need to revise is explicitly realised in the curriculum of Hungary ... half the time-tabled hours in the final year of the gymnasium [for 14–18 year olds] are to be used for systematic recapitulation of the whole course (p.25).

Effective teaching will involve developing metacognition – children learning to know what they know – which is discussed in Chapter 4 and regularly commended throughout the book. One advantage of Rosenshine's method is that it does require the teacher to help children to become aware of what they have learned.

## Subject knowledge

Implicit in this is the view that the teacher has subject-specific expertise (Shulman, 1986). This is a break from some of the past rhetoric which cast the teacher as primarily a facilitator, helping the child to pursue her or his enquiries. The belief was that skills of enquiry were to be valued most, with content being seen as essentially a vehicle for carrying those enquiries along. Yet,

> even in those most student-centred forms of education where much of the initiative is in the hands of students, there is little room for teacher ignorance. Indeed, we have reason to believe that teacher comprehension is even more critical for the inquiry-oriented classroom than for its didactic alternative (Shulman, 1987, p.7).

One of the legacies of past indifference to content knowledge has been teachers who lack a sufficient depth of subject knowledge, even in a core subject such as science.

Subject specialist knowledge has at least three dimensions. The first is knowledge of the content to be covered – of the Maya and of a developing country such as Nigeria, for example. We should not underestimate the difficulty of finding out anything more substantial than 'trivial pursuits' knowledge, although some have naively assumed that a good library is the answer.

The second is a knowledge of what sort of study the subject is. As Wilson and Wineberg (1988) have argued, there are competing views of history, and teaching is influenced by the particular view to which the teacher subscribes. If the teacher has not had to think epistemologically there is a good chance of him acting on the assumption that geography and history are information-gathering subjects and no more.

> Depending on their teachers' orientations, some students may learn that mathematics is an organized body of knowledge to be understood whereas other students might learn that mathematics is a collection of procedures to be memorized (Brophy, 1991, p.351).

The more limited the teacher's grasp of the subject, the more likely is it that there will be an emphasis on the coping strategies of seatwork, routinised work and fact-gathering.

Thirdly teachers' knowledge of an academic subject must be energised by insights into ways in which it might effectively be shared with children. Shulman (1986) called this pedagogical content knowledge, an amalgam of educational and subject matter knowledge. Without that, interesting educational ideas are no more than just ideas. With it there is a better chance that they may be usefully worked through with children. This is the knowledge which lies at the core of teaching, for not only is it the source of ideas for classroom activity, it is also the source of expectations about what children can and should do. There is considerable agreement that too often teachers' expectations are too low and this can be traced back to insufficient pedagogical content knowledge, which means that the teacher is working without fully realising why she is teaching a subject and probably with an inadequate knowledge of the techniques which can be used to challenge children: 'While the academic demands on students tend to be fairly minimal', wrote Anderson and Burns (1989, p.352), 'the greater the emphasis on those demands and students' needs to meet those demands, the greater their achievement in the basic skills'.

Without these three types of subject matter knowledge the teacher's options are severely limited. However, there is a knotty problem identified by McNamara and Pettitt (1991) who considered the copious research into children's errors in subtraction. How useful is such detailed subject matter knowledge? Not very useful, they said, since the research produced too much knowledge and the constraints of the classroom limited teachers' room to apply it. Fair though that point is, we might say that the better thinkers have more options but may not be able to capitalise upon them. For example, Winitzky (1992) has shown that there is a connection between the complexity of teachers' schemata about teaching and their ability to think reflectively about their work. The connection with practice is, she agreed, unclear. This is not the same as saying that teachers' thinking and planning are unimportant topics. The volume of recent research attests the opposite (e.g. Clark and Peterson, 1986). Yet, if we are looking for criteria of teacher effectiveness, beliefs and knowledge will not be sufficient. It is true that a reflective cast of mind is valued, but it is equally true that effective teaching cannot be judged by exhibitions of analytical skill, desirable though it is as a component.

**Classroom management**

What are the characteristics of the practices of effective teachers? Undoubtedly they are good classroom managers and their lessons are characterised by smoothness, pace, busy-ness, a high level of pupil time-on-task, 'withitness' (the teacher seems to have eyes in the back of her head), good working relationships and established routines. Implicit in this is the idea that the classroom is orderly, and there is some agreement that such orderliness is best founded on positive dealings with children – 'The more teachers publicly demean students, the greater the threat to students' self-esteem, and the less willing they are to work' (Rosenholtz, 1991, p.117).

Effective classroom management means that work is structured (the teacher has taken control of the subject matter in a purposeful way), so there is outlining, previewing and summarising (the teacher is connecting what is being learned with what has been learned), and there is feedback to students (Goodlad, 1984; Anderson and Burns, 1989; Brophy, 1991). Effective teachers' lessons are well prepared, which can be seen in the clarity of their exposition and instructions (Kyriacou, 1991), which is related in turn to confidence in subject matter knowledge. A sign of effective teaching is that the children appreciate it.

There are, then, plenty of characteristics which have, at some time, been identified with effective teaching (Brophy and Good, 1986). The problem takes two forms. The first is that there is an excess of correlations, many of which have not proved stable, so that 'differences in individual teaching behaviours are not reliably associated with differences in student achievement' (Anderson and Burns, 1989, p.348). A well-known illustration of this concerns questioning. Often we are told that closed, factual questions are less desirable than open-ended questions of the sort which ask 'why?'. Yet Dillon (1982) contends that teacher questioning is undesirable, while others argue that closed questions are important (D. Hargreaves, 1984; Doyle, 1986). Further evidence of the seriousness of this problem is provided by the IEA study of the relationship between teaching and learning in eight countries.

> Teacher behaviors were more consistently associated with academic *engagement* than with final achievement. Thus, what teachers do in their classrooms appears more highly related to what students *do*, than what they learn. Differences in teacher behaviors are not related to differences in students' achievement (Anderson *et al*, 1989, pp.292–3 – emphases added).

The second form of the problem is that even if one does arrive at some list of factors which can be justified as constituting the most important elements in effective teaching, there remains the formidable task of expressing exactly what those factors mean. So, how is one to distinguish a well-paced lesson from a moderately well-paced lesson, and either from a poorly paced lesson? From whose point of view is one doing the analysis? And how reliable is the judgement? Answers to these questions implicitly represent a theory of effective instruction and of effective learning. Who is to say whether it is a good theory? Consider the work of Cangelosi (1991).

Cangelosi described a project to establish a fair way of evaluating classroom instruction, something which is of concern to academics but which also is a live, practical issue in the guise of teacher appraisal and performance-related pay. Twenty-five per cent of the evaluation score was allocated to goal setting; 35 per cent to classroom management and discipline; 30 per cent to instructional methodology; and 10 per cent to the teacher's assessment of student achievement. It is not clear how these weightings were achieved. The four domains were in turn broken into sub-criteria. Classroom management and discipline was divided into: establishing purposeful, businesslike learning environment (10 per cent); orchestrating smooth, efficient transition periods (3 per cent); obtaining student engagement so that at least 90 per cent are engaged in the initial stages of learning activities (7 per cent); maintaining that level (5 per cent); efficiently teaching students to supplant off-task behaviours with on-task behaviours (10 per cent). In turn the first sub-criterion was split into an evaluation of the learning materials; whether there was a swift despatch of non-learning activities; whether teacher talk and actions contributed to, rather than detracted from the learning activity; and whether respectful behaviours were modelled and motivated.

We might object to the positivist assumptions (the way that a theory of teaching is presented neutrally, almost as common sense) and to the assumptions which are made about the normal way of educating a diversity of children in a range of areas. There is also the problem that implicit in this factoral approach is the idea that teaching can be broken down into lists of competences, much as learning was once broken down into lists of objectives. Just as the objectives approach to learning was found to be practically deficient, educationally unhelpful and philosophically bankrupt (see, for example Stenhouse, 1975, ch.5), so too the idea that teaching can be defined as a fistful of competences is open to objection. The very idea of professionalism presupposes an area of independent, spontaneous, creative action, and Rosenholtz has argued that preserving that freedom is important if teachers are to give of their best. There is also a suspicion that these systems define effectiveness in terms of the measurable, and not in terms of the desirable. Furthermore, the teacher is rendered powerless in the face of a top down definition of effectiveness, and the fact that it may have a research basis just adds insult to injury, becoming another example of the way research often works against teachers. Lastly, research into correlates of effective teaching will necessarily sift out those factors which are exceptions to the trend and produce a statistically derived set of norms. As norms, they reflect convergences in the figures, but they certainly do not describe the *range* of factors associated with good teaching. Applying those norms with a view to improving standards is statistically naive and liable to be counter-productive.

A lack of historical awareness can also lead us to take for granted the characteristics of good teaching, treating them as common-sense 'givens' rather than as problematic social constructs. Notions of good practice are labile, the product not just of a time but also of the culture of a place. Teachers in France have very different views of their jobs and different ways of working, emphasising whole class, didactic methods in the pursuit of the acquisition of unproblematic knowledge (DES, 1991d; Osborn and Broadfoot, 1992). There are obviously some common characteristics of teaching, things such as being prepared, being able to maintain order and getting children to engage with the work, but the forms which these take and the standards to be applied vary sharply, reflecting ideologies about education, children and teachers. These ideologies may, according to Alexander (1984; 1992a), be an obstacle to the improvement of primary education.

A fundamental issue in the definition of good teaching is whether it is competence or performance that is being judged. Performance will often fall short of competence, and generally does so, for example, when I teach. The reasons for this are many, but it is helpful to group them into two sets. One set comprises elements which are part and parcel of the individual – declining intellect, lack of stamina, addictions, disenchantment with teaching. The other set takes in all the external, contextual factors which limit performance. Here the design of the classroom (which may stop the teacher from supervising all the children), or the number of children in the class (which may cause overcrowding), or the composition of the class (which may include children with special educational needs), or the provision of learning resources (which may be inadequate), can all affect the quality of teaching.

But context is human as well as physical, a theme which pervaded Chapter 2. Work on total quality management (Oakland, 1989), has emphasised the importance of values and attitudes to the success of an organisation. Rosenholtz echoed that in writing of some older teachers that 'after a time the emptiness of teachers' professional growth becomes a numb ache felt in students' learning opportunities' (1991, p.100). Nias and her colleagues (1992) observed that primary teachers want to work in an adult environment in which they share educational beliefs, extend their professional thinking through social intercourse, and where help, sympathy and friendship are available. In learning enriched schools, where teachers feel valued, where they are positive about their work and chances of helping children to learn, and where they collaborate to develop their understandings of education, in such schools, the context supports good teaching. And good teaching vivifies the school.

Similarly, the culture of the school may engender routine or poor performances through emphasising bureaucratic accountability, through a culture of individualism or of 'balkanisation' (Hargreaves, 1992), through a pathological view of children and their parents, or through a belief that teachers are powerless in the face of multiple constraints. Changing the 'Hill Street staffroom' is one of the hardest and most urgent tasks in education, and one of the most intractable, since it means changing people who have got into a mind set which prevents good teaching.

Of course, being positive and having a lively, enquiring mind do not guarantee that one will teach well, but add to these dispositions the collegiality which can only come with confidence in self (and not from imposed co-operation, although that may be a starting point), and the critical mass of the school effect can transform the possible. It must still be said that meagre resources can hobble these positive factors, but meagreness is, in a very real sense, in the eyes of the beholder.

Knowledge, classroom management skills and a lively, enquiring mind all contribute to effective teaching. But not only is good practice, the criterion of teaching effectiveness, a contested concept (Alexander, 1992), but also the evidence is that there are several ways of teaching to embody good practice. That is not to say that we cannot recognise cases of effective teaching, but rather to say that our judgement is not infallible. With that reservation in mind, I conclude this discussion with a list of six principles of effective teaching. They relate to higher education but I am quoting them because they reinforce the basic message of these opening chapters, that it is values and people which determine the quality of education and that it is important to keep on learning by evaluating what we do when we teach.

Principle 1.  Interest and explanation ... Even more important than clear explanation would appear to be the related ability to make the material of a subject genuinely interesting.

Principle 2.  Concern and respect for students and student learning .... Good teaching is nothing to do with making things hard ... It is everything to do with benevolence and humility.

Principle 3.  Appropriate assessment and feedback.

Principle 4.  Clear goals and intellectual challenge.  Research into effective schooling overwhelmingly shows that consistently high academic expectations are associated with high levels of pupil performance.

Principle 5.  Independence, control and active engagement.

Principle 6.  Learning from students ... Effective teaching refuses to take its effect on students for granted.  It sees the relation between teaching and learning as problematic, uncertain and relative.  Good teaching is open to change; it involves constantly trying to find out what its effects are on learning and modifying it in the light of evidence collected (Ramsden, 1993, p.45–7).

*Chapter 4*

# Children

## Children and development

Once children were seen as adults in miniature, marked by Man's original sin, which was to be driven out in order to save their souls. Love was not alien to that concept of childhood but foreign to it was the notion that childhood was a distinctive and special thing, qualitatively different from adulthood. That view of childhood as a distinctive and special phase developed fitfully and falteringly, until in the early twentieth century it had some currency among some intellectuals. I want to point to the particular contribution of one of them, Jean Piaget, who argued that intellectual growth through childhood – and thereafter – involved the restructuring of the mind which qualitatively changed the child's ways of thinking and understanding. For him children were not to be seen as deficient when compared to adults but as quite different in their mental life. The 'children as little adults' view was rejected.

In this section I shall not try to say what children of different ages are like, nor what they can do. Instead, I want to outline some of the salient principles to have in mind when we think about children learning.

Four of Piaget's ideas have been particularly influential. First, there is his insistence, drawn from Darwinism, that development is an *active* process, not a passive one, such as physical growth is. Unfortunately, Piaget's notion of activity, which plainly related to mental activity, has been widely trivialised as physical activity, as though children were the molluscs which Piaget began his scientific career by studying. A second key idea was that thinking develops in a series of stages, which follow an invariant order. Thirdly, the demonstration that each stage could be associated with a certain mental age, so that a mental age of eight typically went with the concrete operational stage, while a mental age of four was associated with the pre-operational stage. Fourthly, the claim that there was a unity about stages, so that whatever the content which a learner encountered, the highest level of thinking available would be set by the learner's stage. So, a nine year old could use pre-operational or concrete operational thinking, but the later, formal operational thought would not be available to her.

Piaget had little time for 'the American question', that is whether the process of development may be accelerated. There is no doubt that children can be trained to appear as if they have precociously mastered stages of thinking, but Piaget's interest was not in whether separated signs of mastery could be found, but more in whether the thinking characteristic of a stage had been consolidated and generalised. A further difficulty with Piaget's ideas is his (often ignored) insistence that he was trying to discover how knowledge developed in children's minds, not to offer educational propositions. Consequently, those who have tried to adapt his ideas to education have had to do so without the benefit of principles to shape their adaptation. Some of these adaptations have been far from convincing, and there is a sense in which much of the argument about the correctness of Piaget's theories may be reduced to argument over ways of applying them to educational settings.

Piaget emphasised the effect of the social environment in children's development, seeing both social interaction and language as significant. He did not, however, give them the priority which the Russian psychologist Vygotsky (1962) accorded them. While in agreement with Piaget on many points (as Piaget was with him), Vygotsky is usually remembered for three ideas. The first is that language has the power to shape future mental development – it is not simply the product of the mind's structures but something which can itself shape them. Secondly, he insisted on social interaction as a prime way in which people learn, which is often expressed in his phrase that what the child can do co-operatively today she will be able to do individually tomorrow. Thirdly, he coined the phrase 'zone of proximal development' (ZPD) to describe the area of thinking which lay at, or just beyond, the learner's most advanced, current understanding. Targeting activities in this zone was a powerful way of promoting development, he argued. Implicit in his psychology is a Marxist dialectic and a view of progress, which is expressed in Vygotsky's underlying belief that education could accelerate development.

The major area of contention about Piaget's ideas takes up a different aspect of stage theories. He argued that there was a unity to a stage, but there is a considerable amount of research which seems to show that development is uneven, with children operating now at this stage, now at another. The meaning of these studies is open to vigorous dispute, but there is a common view that learning may be seen as domain specific, rather than as generic. In other words, ways of thinking are not cross-curricular but subject specific, to use an educational metaphor. In one domain – science and maths – I may have a good grasp of the rules and routines of procedure and be operating at a high level, while in another domain – learning a foreign language, for example – I may be baffled by apparently unrelated streams of vocabulary and grammatical whimsies. This domain-specific approach has stimulated a lot of research into the problems of learning-specific subject matter, into the ways in which children do (mis)learn and (mis)apply subject understandings, and into what children actually *can* achieve. Crudely, this may be compared with the developmental work of Piaget which often seemed to emphasise what children *could not* do in general.

Research into the contextual variables which affect the success with which problems are solved shows the problems of the transfer of learning. Good examples of this literature may be found in the field of child development where there have been vigorous arguments about the age at which learners can perform certain tasks and show characteristics of a certain stage. A popular strategy has been to take original Piagetian tasks and change the way they are presented so as to make them more homely and less abstract. Donaldson (1978) has provided a good summary of this line of research. Similarly in mathematics, where O' Reilly (1990) argued that task-specific variables exerted such an influence in assessment tasks that it is futile to talk of hierarchies of difficulty of mathematical concepts: all that could be said was that certain tasks were more difficult than certain others, and that there is no guarantee that two tasks assessing the same concept would be of similar difficulty.

In other words, the application of principles and the transfer of training do not appear to be commonplace, successful features of intellectual life.

Fruitful though this domain-specific developmental psychology is proving, it is not a pedagogical panacea (McNamara and Pettitt, 1991), since it gives teachers far more to learn and remember as it replaces simple notions of stages with sheafs of data about children's developing understanding in each school subject. Moreover, the concept of the child as a bundle of domain-specific competences is patently lacking something, for however ragged might be the pattern of development, there is a certain, unifying nine-year-oldness about nine year olds.

Moreover, some researchers have argued that certain programmes can promote general intellectual development, thereby questioning the domain-specific premise. A notable example of this in the high school years has been the Cognitive Advancement in Science Education programme (Adey *et al*, 1990), which showed that teaching science in a fashion which encouraged children to develop general reasoning strategies and concepts was associated with cross-curricular improvement in their academic performance. Smith and Knight (1992) have said that some aspects of high school children's displays of history reasoning are of the same order of development as their levels of formal operational reasoning, which calls into question earlier, domain-specific research saying that formal operational thinking in history develops much later than formal operational thinking in general (see also Booth, 1979; West, 1981).

Here it is not necessary to attempt to resolve these positions. It suffices to draw the uncontentious conclusion that a knowledge of children's typical modes of thinking needs to be supplemented by an awareness of the peculiarities of developing understanding in different subject curricula.

This highly compressed account has advanced the following propositions:

- children's learning entails mental activity – to learn they need to work on the material which they are processing;
- this will often involve setting work which is in the ZPD;
- at first children *may* need to tackle such work collaboratively;
- there are both general elements in learning and domain-specific ones – both need to be borne in mind;
- an implication of the domain-specific perspective is that something learned in one domain may not easily transfer to another.

## Children as learners

Stories of child development do not tell the whole tale about learning. Four other important elements are discussed in this section.

### Motivation

The research picture of primary classrooms is one of happy busyness and in the main, motivation is not a problem in these circumstances, although Doyle (1983) has argued that one reason for this is that children have succeeded in bargaining for the sort of classroom in which the way to get rewards is well known, where ambiguity and uncertainty are minimised, and where *effort* is rewarded.

Piaget, who is often portrayed as interested only in logical puzzles, said that affectivity – the emotions and feelings – were related to cognition just as gasoline was related to the motor car: thinking needed feeling, or in this case motivation (Piaget, 1981). Just as a car might lack gasoline, this simile reminds us that children might lack motivation to learn. However, theories of motivation have seemed to be rather better at rationalising why some children fail to work than at giving teachers any way of predicting and controlling children's motivation. Platitudes about interest, engagement, discovery and relevance abound, often in sublime indifference to the multiple meanings those ideas carry and to the way that what interests one child bores another; what one teacher vivifies, another smothers.

A more promising line has been described by Rogers (1990), who has argued that an essential aspect of motivation lies in children's attributions of success and failure. Taking the premise that we try to maintain our self-esteem, he noted several strategies for doing so. One is to try to control the situation so that threats, such as intellectually demanding work – do not arise. This may explain why children have a vested interest in the happy routine of primary schooling. Another strategy depends on attributing failure to lack of effort. All the time that it is possible to believe that indifferent performance is remediable by greater effort on the grounds that it was mainly lack of effort which caused the indifferent performance, it is possible for the learner to maintain a benign disposition to schooling, since the only sense in which self-esteem has been threatened is in the moral sense that the learner could be accused of not having worked hard enough. Since that is culturally acceptable, the attribution protects the learner from the consequences of poor performance and their motivation need not be corroded.

Where, on the other hand, learned helplessness has set in and the child attributes poor performance to some fixed failing in himself, there is no incentive, no motivation to try to make things better. Indeed, there is every reason to do less and to be disruptive in order that the occasions for failure are reduced or even cancelled out by acquiring a reputation among other children as a counter-cultural hero.

In order to maintain motivation, it follows that teachers should try to emphasise the room for improvement; to associate improvement with effort; to support efforts so that success is seen; and to avoid, at all costs, acting as if a child's potential has been fixed, reached and derided.

## Orderliness

Learning demands orderliness, although orderliness cannot be a sufficient condition for learning to take place. Sammons and Mortimore (1990) have provided powerful evidence that where children make good academic progress, then their behaviour also tends to be good. The converse is also true, that frustration at not learning leads the child to act in ways which schools are likely to see as disruptive. Fostering good behaviour, then, is as much a curriculum issue as a discipline one.

When it comes to treating disorderliness, a considerable amount of emphasis has been put on positive behaviour management techniques (e.g. Wheldall and Merrett, 1984). The teacher needs to identify the antecedents of the problem behaviour and to estimate its size or incidence. Treatment should be aimed at encouraging desirable behaviours, not at harrying the problem behaviour, which will begin to wilt. Although there is plenty of scope for scepticism about this approach, there is also a plentiful literature attesting to its effectiveness as a way of dealing with individual, problem behaviours. 'The more teachers publicly demean students, the greater threat to students' self-esteem, and the less willing they are to work' – or to conform (Rosenholtz, 1991, p.117).

A similar approach has involved giving children responsibility through negotiation of working procedures and rules with them. Again, it has been seen as productive to frame rules which accentuate the positive, rather than to produce substantial lists of banned deeds.

Finally, as primary schools take more seriously the business of working with parents, benefits may be seen in the classroom.

## Individual differences

So obvious are individual differences that strenuous attempts have been made to individualise primary schooling: not, it has been said, with notable success (Thomas, 1992). Here, five sorts of difference are added to those in motivation and behaviour which have already been noticed.

It follows from Piaget and Vygotsky's interpretation of the learner as a meaning-maker that,

> every learner creates his or her own knowledge in a somewhat idiosyncratic manner ... New information is perceived and interpreted in a more-or-less unique manner based on the learner's previous knowledge and other factors ... the learner must elaborate the new information and relate it to other information ... due to the constructive nature of meaningful learning, no two students have exactly the same perception of the instructional situation or end up with exactly the same understanding of the material being acquired (Shuell, 1992).

This insight has been influential in science teaching (Harlen and Osborne, 1985) but has had surprisingly little impact in those value-saturated fields where it might be predicted that children's knowledge and learning would tend even more strongly towards the idiosyncratic. This is discussed further in Chapter 6, where it is argued that the old saw that teachers should begin with what the learner already knows and can do needs to be more sharply recognised. In particular, teachers need to make or have some prior, fair estimate of children's special understanding of the topics to be encountered.

A second form of difference is less easy to handle. That there are different learning styles is widely recognised. Where one child is field dependent, focusing on the detail of the case in hand, another is not, and may make links, transfer information and ideas and reflect on the activity itself. There are other ways of describing differences in learning style, for example as differences between convergent and divergent thinkers, between surface and deep processing, or between logical and lateral thinkers. For each pair, one of the ways of thinking is the more highly prized. Can those styles be taught, or are they relatively stable and impervious? Certainly, there are programmes designed to encourage critical thinking, to provide philosophy for children, or to help people to become lateral thinkers. Their efficacy is contested.

As so often when examining children's learning, teaching principles cannot be read off from the findings. Is it desirable to promote one style of learning rather than another? In all subjects and in all circumstances? The subject matter of the humanities would seem well matched to divergent, lateral, field-independent, deep-processing styles, but of course that implies that the child has gained certain knowledge in the first place. And that these ways of thinking can be fostered. Research which has a basis in the primary curriculum and which addresses these individual differences is scarce.

The matter of differences in achievement and ability is also pressing now that children's humanities work is to be assessed and reported in its own right and may well become an important vehicle for assessing and reporting language achievements. It has been reported (Bennett *et al*, 1984) that teachers matched maths and reading work to children's capability about a third of the time. The possibility that this is a good performance has hardly been discussed, with more attention being paid to findings that the less able were given work that was too hard (see also Desforges and Cockburn, 1987) and the more able, work that was too easy.

There are intractable problems surrounding this concept of 'match'. For example, practice activities might be suitable when a child had got the gist of a new concept or procedure, but inappropriate once that concept or procedure had become well tuned (Case, 1985). At such a point Vygotsky's concept of the ZPD implies that the work should be a little too hard for the learner to manage simply – it might need a collaborative effort to get to grips with the task, and certainly the teacher should ensure that this work was neither aimless nor unsupported.

In short, it is one thing to identify a range of ability in children but another thing to know what to do about it. The demand that children and their work should be better matched is common sense but raises the most awkward of questions about the structure of knowledge and the ways in which people learn. In these circumstances it has to be asked whether a bad map of children's cognitive development (an example of which is the English National Curriculum) is better than no map at all. Preferring the latter may lead straight back to an 'exposure' approach to the humanities, where material was presented to children in an undifferentiated manner, and each interpreted it according to her own ability. Yet, I do not know of research into matching humanities tasks to children, which leaves teachers between instinctive matching and the indifference of exposure.

Two other significant differences among learners, namely differences in culture and in gender, share certain features. Both are socially constructed distinctions, both are often assumed to be of no practical significance, each has been met with the response that in treating all children alike the difference has been fairly dealt with, but in both cases there are significant educational consequences.

There are at least four claims about how schooling should respond to the fact of multi-racial societies in a multi-racial world. One is that children should have the chance to celebrate their identity in their schooling; curriculum content should be multi-racial. The second is that stereotypes about other races should be excised from the curriculum, which should encourage human understanding as a fundamental goal. This would obviously extend to the pastoral curriculum and to relations among the children, parents and staff as a whole. Anti-racist teaching is a third method which involves outright assaults on the racist innuendo in schooling and society at large. The contrary position asserts that schools should assimilate children – the melting pot thesis – that society is not racist, and that children should be inducted into the mainstream culture (Milner, 1983).

Whatever stance is adopted, it is particularly important to recognise that the humanities depend on children making an attempt to understand other people's actions and ways of life, no matter how very different these actions and states may be from their own. Sometimes called empathy, it is not only fundamental to the humanities but it is also a disposition which is central to inter-cultural understanding, the lynch-pin of a sensitive regard for people of other races and religions today. Promoting this attitude of trying to understand people in the past and in the present as if one were standing in their shoes is a necessary part of teaching the humanities and one of its most valuable outcomes.

These arguments are replicated in the field of gender, where it is claimed that subjects have been constructed in a masculine form; that girls are ignored in the classroom, getting less attention from the teacher and fewer opportunities to talk in mixed-sex discussion; that they begin compulsory schooling with superior achievements to males but end it as inferior; and that their self-images and the general projection of women are both stereotyped and negative, embodying male hegemony.

In the humanities this critique needs to be particularly carefully studied. More collaborative work may disadvantage more deferential girls, who, in any case, do well on written tasks. The depictions of people in other places and times are often marked by first, an absence of women, and secondly by a message that women were – or are – marginal. Now, it has to be recognised that such has indeed been the case in the past, and is so in some parts of the world today. A response is that girl-fair teaching involves examining the absence or subservience of women, explicitly comparing then and there with now. Ironically, this may prove unpopular with parents of some non-European racial origins. A vexing conclusion is that education which is sensitive to some individual differences is upsetting to others whose differences are different. More attention to girls means less to boys (but boys already get most of teachers' attention); to slower learners at the expense of the gifted; to the Third World means that children will not learn about their own country; helping children with misconceptions to construct better ideas may be at the expense of stimulating those with better-formed concepts. And so on.

*Learning strategies*

In the USA Slavin (1990) has vigorously developed co-operative learning methods and has argued that impressive learning outcomes can result. Reviewing 60 studies which were regarded as sufficiently rigorous, he found that his preferred group-work methods showed a statistically significant, general, positive effect on children's cognitive learning. In addition, he said that

> the overall effects of cooperative learning on student self-esteem, peer support for achievement, internal locus of control, time on task, liking of class and classmates, and other variables are positive and robust (1990, p.53).

There are several ways of explaining these effects. The work of Piaget emphasised that learning is a social activity and the business of sharing views, of having them challenged by others, and of trying to sustain them can all help to provoke that restructuring of thought which characterises development. Vygotsky took a similar line, famously arguing that what children could do collaboratively today they might do individually tomorrow. In this account, collaboration is a route to autonomy. Lastly, there is the old observation that to teach is to learn twice, so that where a child has to explain something to another the act of elaborating the connections and meanings in the material both clarifies it for the 'teacher' and facilitates its storage in and later retrieval from long-term memory.

Yet, as we shall see in Chapters 6 and 8, whatever the proclaimed benefits of group-work, we should not forget that children tend to work in groups but not as groups (Galton, 1989). Attempts in England to improve the quality of group-work have not been successful (Bennett *et al*, 1984; Galton, 1989). Galton and Williamson (1992) have argued that children need to have considerable confidence to do group-work successfully, since it is hard for them to work in groups with the security of knowing that they are 'getting it right', doing what the teacher wants (which is their main goal), so as to avoid reprimand. They also reported that children were more happy with group-work which was practical rather than that which involved discussion, which is rather bad news for the humanities. They reported difficulties in trying to get teachers to be more effective at group-work, concluding with a number of observations on the process of teacher professional development and on action research, observations which are discussed in Chapters 1 and 11. A final point, again with strong implications for the humanities, is that Slavin's stimulating but complex techniques appear to be most fully developed for those aspects of schooling which trade in fact and certainty.

Increasingly psychologists are showing an interest in metacognition, which may be described as helping children to be conscious of what they know and can do and then teaching them how to draw purposefully upon that knowledge and to deploy it when working on problems. There is, then, a difference between, say, the skills of doing something and the more general 'executive strategies', which, where they exist, are used to deploy those 'lower level' skills appropriately, efficiently and effectively.

Metacognition may be compared to teaching a child carpentry. The child may know what she wants to make or shape, and can make progress through banging, gouging, nailing, cutting and the like. Play, which this is, in a sense is important at all ages. However, if she comes to know what the tools in the carpentry set can do she is better placed to exercise a range of options in her work; if, in addition, she is aware of a range of techniques, such as screwing, glueing, making joints, then her options are further increased. She can select from tools and techniques those she thinks best suited to her purpose. That is not to say that the selection will always be judicious, nor that the product will necessarily be felicitous. However, the possibilities have been improved through metacognitive carpentry. We shall return to this issue in Chapter 6, in the context of geography.

So, in their humanities work children should:

- be encouraged to think metacognitively;
- be given opportunities to work together;
- sometimes be given work which is rather hard for them;
- face work which may corrode stereotypical thinking;
- have their misconceptions taken into account when the teacher plans a topic;
- be encouraged to explore the reasons why people live and act (or lived and acted) as they do;
- see a link between their efforts and their achievements, and not

　　　learn to attribute performance to personal inadequacy;
● be praised and be interested;
● be encouraged to extend humanities (domain-specific) thinking to
　　　other subjects.

## Children, teaching and schools – an overview

In these four chapters we have skimmed through some research findings
which should warn us that it is entirely inadequate to consider primary
geography and primary history in isolation. It may be that developing a
new humanities curriculum is a good way of bringing a staff together
and creating that sense of working together as a whole school which is
so important for effective education. Alternatively, it may be that such a
sense of purpose already exists, and that consideration of the humanities
curriculum instead provides a way for colleagues to start examining
their teaching and learning practices in an action research manner, doing
so in an area of the curriculum which has traditionally been marginal
and where, as a result, teachers are less likely to feel that their
professional credibility is at stake. What is clear, however, is that an
effective humanities curriculum is bound up with a number of other
things. It is related to the effectiveness of the school, and we have
noticed the importance of leadership, reflection and a positive
disposition amongst staff who get along with each other. We have also
seen how effective humanities work presumes effective teaching
methods. Indeed, there is no one way to be an effective teacher, but
there are a number of points of agreement about the range of ways of
working that will tend to be effective. And lastly, looking at the learner
has made it clear that hack humanities – hurling trivial content around in
the hope that children might catch some of it – is entirely inappropriate.
Effective learning cannot be left to chance. Children need to be engaged
in structured and purposeful work which takes a diversity of forms.
　　　Underpinning these thoughts has been the notion that the teacher can
be a good student of her own practice, using an action research approach
as a way of enquiring systematically into ways of doing better. This is
particularly relevant in the early 1990s when national curricula have
imposed new content and new standards on schools and, at a stroke,
rendered redundant much earlier research which was premised upon a
very different world. As a result, there is a strong sense in which
knowledge is now in the hands of the teachers – both as the people who

are daily making the new curricula and as the people who are daily, in their actions, researching into it.

With these general points in mind we can turn to primary geography and primary history.

# Chapter 5

# The Nature of Geography

## The discipline

Different ideas about the nature of a subject, about its constituent elements, concepts, ways of establishing propositions, procedures and criteria of value lead to different ways of teaching it. The suggestion that school subjects should mirror, albeit imperfectly and dimly, the mature disciplines by introducing children to those disciplines' characteristic ways of thinking and working, has only confirmed this link between the teacher's understanding of the adult study and the way in which the school subject is handled. So, consideration of primary geography needs to be related to an understanding of the academic discipline, not on the assumption that the former must perfectly reflect the latter, but rather on the assumption that they are both part of the same family, having things in common as well as things which distinguish them from each other.

One of the principal tasks of geography, in its early days was, in the words of Bradbeer (1991, p.13) 'to synthesise the growing body of information about the earth, its natural features and its peoples'. Here physical geography and human geography met, and no-where was this better seen than in the USA where geography was dominated by environmental determinism, that is, by the view that physical geography shaped human life and that geography was a scientific account of the regularities in this relationship (Smith, 1989). In the inter-war years this gave way to regional studies, or chorology. Regional studies, in which all knowledge of a place was drawn together, were defined as geography's distinctive feature but since these studies tended to be descriptive, they were faulted for providing 'no more than a superficial analysis, and the division of labour within the discipline, whereby people specialised on different areas of the earth was both inefficient and ineffective' (Johnston, 1991, p.51). The definition of a 'region' was also problematic. Moreover, this distinctiveness has been seen as cutting geography off from the main stream of social science, leaving it with the interstices between other, more vigorous disciplines (Smith, 1989). Developments passed geography by.

Discontent with the inter-war regional studies led to the adoption of hypotheses-testing and the statistical tools of natural science in the mid-twentieth century. This, known as the quantitative revolution, took place in conjunction with the burgeoning of analytical, systematic studies, in which a theme, such as urban location or land transport systems, was pursued across regions, usually with a view to inducing some form of generalisation or law. This positivist, 'scientific' form of geography is still strong and well represented in professional journals, but it has been criticised in its turn, particularly on the grounds that it took the human element out of geography, reducing people to variables within equations. The critics argued that what mattered was not so much the objectivity of measured distance, for example, but rather people's perceptions of distance. A shopping centre might lie close to a housing area, objectively, but separated by a major road system the two might subjectively be further apart than the shopping centre and a more distant area with better links. This search for understanding of the meanings which people ascribed to the spatial dimensions of their lives aligned geography with other social studies. The most distinctive thing about geography became its concern with the human, spatial dimension – in which respect it is not unique, although it may be pre-eminent.

Where geographers of the inter-war years, such as Hartshorne, had sought to keep geography and history separate, in post-war years there developed an interest in the dynamics of change in space:

> the same old suspicion that time should be left to historians has cropped up again – even reinforced in some discussions by a feeling that 'time' is some kind of hostile concept, challenging the 'space' of geography for supremacy. But *both* dimensions are essential to *all* kinds of study (Chappell, 1989, p.18).

> I still insist that all geography is necessarily historical geography, that a concern with genesis and spatio-temporal processes of social transformation must dominate over pure description of spatial patterns (Harvey, 1989, p.212) .

Notice not only the historical emphasis on change, but also the idea that geography is a study of the social world, a sharp contrast to the environmental determinism of the turn of the century. Geography has become essentially human geography.

A consequence has been uncertainty about the status of physical geography. Whether physical geography has much in common with human geography is disputable. Johnston (1991, p.viii) wrote that,

> I find the links between physical and human geography tenuous as those disciplines are currently practised. The major link between them is the sharing of techniques and research procedures, but these are shared with other disciplines too.

Whether growing environmental concern will bring the two sorts of geography closer together remains to be seen, for there are fears (Macmillan, 1989) that the natural sciences will capture physical geography and complete geography's transformation from a physical to a social science. The same argument about territory surfaced in 1990 in the making of the school geography curriculum for England.

Geography does not exist just as a 'pure' study, of the same sort as is medieval history, since it has strength in applied forms, and it has had particular influence in various fields of planning, of which town and country planning is the most obvious. Monitoring and describing the socially constructed variations of space, for example the distribution of various forms of ill-health, of educational achievements, and of female, part-time work, are other manifestations of applied geography. Yet this concern of geography is threatened in those developed countries which have entered a 'post-welfarist' phase (Bennett, 1989) in which planning and notions of equality are being replaced by market forces and notions of liberty. Human geography's claim to be important because it is an applied subject is weakened if free markets have no time for its planning insights.

Recently there has been a revival of interest in specific *locales*, not as a revival of the old regional geographies with their emphasis on unanalytical description, but in the recognition that different locations do differ, and that those differences are analytically significant. 'Geography today', claimed Cosgrove (1989, p.243) 'celebrates diversity and particularly contextual studies of locale: historical and cultural reconstruction and a revived description'. While Cosgrove is not without critics (Macmillan, 1989), there is agreement that places, understood as sites of human, social and economic activity, are important as units of analysis, much as in history understanding depends on the match between explanations and particular events.

The resulting picture is of an area of study which is characterised by a variety of competing and sometimes contradictory definitions. Geography may indeed be a synthesising subject, but it is far from clear what it is synthesising that makes it different from other social studies. 'From there', commented Bennett (1989, p.280), 'it is but a short step to argue that geography should be de-defined'. The claim that spatial relationships are distinctive of geography may be true but it may also be trite. It is hard to think of any study of people which is not also, in principle, interested in the way that things vary across space. This picture is one of a subject which occupies 'an already fragmented field', and where examination of the history of the subject 'has not had the effect of building a consensus about the practices of the discipline' (Entrikin, 1989, p.5) – if it can be called a discipline.

Not that this is remarkable, let alone reprehensible, as work on the development of school subjects has indicated. Goodson (1988) has argued that philosophical analyses of knowledge are flawed since they simply celebrate

> a *fait accompli* in the evolution of a discipline and associated school subject. What is left unexplained are the stages of evolution towards this position and the forces which push aspiring academic subjects to follow similar routes (p.164).

He suggests that subjects are defined by their practitioners as much as by epistemology, that is to say that, sociologically speaking, geography is what those people who are recognised as geographers do. This society of geographers embraces a range of practices and positions, a range which is both defended and changing. Subjects, then, are not static but, as he shows with reference to the interplay between school geography and academic geography, in constant flux. Dominant positions may be identified, and he showed how the geographical hegemony defended itself against the fledgling environmental studies (Goodson, 1983).

On this view it is naive to expect consensus of definition not just in geography but in any subject. The possibility remains, however, that geography's identity crisis is especially acute. Its concern with place is distinctive but not unique, while its concern with the natural world is shared with science, as are some aspects of its concern with the way in which people interact with their surroundings, through farming (agriculture), construction (civil engineering) and pollution (chemistry).

With religion, ethics, sociology, political science and history it shares a (moral) interest in human lifestyles. As one synthesis of these subjects geography can be regarded as an integrated study in its own right, as a cross-curricular subject.

In summary, four points are worth emphasising. First, we should think not so much of geography as of geographies. We might then expect different views of the subject to lead to rather different educational emphases. Secondly, the view of geography as maps and facts is, on any reckoning, a narrow misrepresentation. Thirdly, geography does not look very much like a subject, in the sense that Hirst (1965) defined a subject, but it is a well-established and productive field of study. Fourthly, it follows that geography draws upon and integrates other subjects: the geographer is a multi-disciplinary person.

As a boundary-breaking subject, and as a bridge between the natural sciences and the arts, geography has a distinctiveness. As a narrowed subject it simply has rivals who may claim to do the job better.

## The primary school study

### Its growth

Readers of Graves' 1975 book *Geography in Education* might have concluded that geography had little place in the primary school, at that level being just

> a coherent way of helping the child unfold those concepts and that conceptualization of space which would develop in a haphazard way through the child's own personal experience. Perhaps geography also begins to hint at those man-land relationships and spatial regularities which will be elaborated in the secondary school (p.206).

He had little else to say about the elementary years, beyond reporting a little research into primary phase children's developing concepts and misconceptions. Even the much more positive view of Norwood relates only to secondary schooling (1943, cit Goodson, 1983, p.67).

> I therefore want to make the bold claim that geography is an essential part of education, whatever forms education may take ... more important than a foreign language or science ... for the simple reason ... that the intelligent person must understand something about the world and the country and the district in which he is set to live his life.

Where Graves observed that it was not easy to identify geographical work in the primary curriculum, it is now there as a foundation subject in England and Wales. In Scotland it is prominent in *Environmental Studies 5–14* (Scottish Office, 1992), while in both the USA and New Zealand there have been attempts to disentangle it from the social studies skein which has apparently somehow hidden the threads of geography.

*Its nature*

What, intellectually, is this school geography which is emerging?

In England, the National Curriculum defines what is currently to count as geography (DES, 1991b). In essence the English National Curriculum requires that primary school children will study:

- A range of geographical skills, particularly ones to do with mapping, so that by the age of 11 most children will be able to: use four figure grid references, use the eight points of the compass, measure straight-line distance on a map, interpret and use symbols, and make maps themselves. They should also be able to observe geographical features and conditions using simple instruments such as clinometers, stopwatches, compasses and thermometers, and be able to locate and select relevant information from atlases, charts, books, globes and computer databases.

- Some children will also be expected to use six figure grid references, longitude and latitude; to interpret relief maps, use distribution patterns and recognise that a globe may be projected as a flat surface.

- In their first two years they should study their own locality and others, both within and beyond England. A context is provided by a simplified map of the UK and one of the world, which between them identify well over 50 geographical features. However, apart from the prescription implied by these maps, the precise areas of study are not laid down, so schools may choose.

- The local study at this level involves children identifying features, land use, journeys and transport systems, the provision of goods and services, the range of leisure and work activities. More skilled children will begin to suggest reasons for migration, and consider the different ways in which things are transported, location and land-use.

● Environmental geography in Years 1 and 2 includes work on the materials which are obtained from the environment, change in the environment, and children's likes and dislikes about the environment.

● These children also carry out landscape and climate studies.

● Additionally, children in Key Stage 2 (Years 3–6) have to work on more detailed maps of the UK and of the world, studying a locality in a developing country and, if they are working for level 5, as a sizeable minority will be, they are to study another country of the European Community. The locality should also be seen in the context of the home region, thereby introducing the concept of 'regions'. Similarities and differences with other areas studied should be brought out and the issue of change should also be woven through the work.

● The interaction of weather, landscape and wealth on people's lives is to be studied in the developing country.

● The physical geography involves them learning about a number of features (beach, river, valley), erosion and deposition processes, water courses, weather conditions in different parts of the world, vulcanology, seismology, and the nature of different soils.

● Settlements and their functions are associated with ideas explaining different population densities and migration and transport patterns, with the most advanced children being encouraged to consider the factors which make for change in human geography, alongside elementary locational theory.

● They are not so explicitly invited to consider the values issues in the environment, although there is considerable emphasis on ways of improving the locality. Global environmental issues get scant attention.

Criticisms of this curriculum remind us that it is simply one view of geography (e.g. Catling, 1990b; Graves *et al*, 1990). A vocal criticism has been that geography can be seen very much as the study of human behaviour, and so it is necessarily, primarily concerned with human values, firstly, in order to make sense of and to understand human action, and secondly, in order to help students reflect upon their own values and the sort of world which they wish to live in (Fisher and Hicks, 1985; Pike and Selby, 1988; Hicks and Steiner, 1989). This curriculum is thought to have pushed values issues to the margins. The choice of content has been seen to encourage the study of the physical nature of places at the expense of the deeply human, value-full study of social, economic and political issues which are connected to them (Morris, 1992).

Unease has also been expressed about the break with the earlier, predominantly local, environmental geography and there is concern that the content specified by the prescribed maps might be excessive and could lead teachers to work didactically to promote 'capes and bays' geography at the expense of the understanding and enquiry skills which are widely seen as central to school geography. Associated with that is a worry that the content could lend itself to a revival of environmental determinism. The rejoinder (Walford, 1991) that enquiry skills are hardly special to geography and would make a poor foundation for its claim to be a discrete subject has force. It has also been argued that there is no reason why teachers should not examine social, economic and political differences between places in the UK and overseas: what the National Curriculum does not prohibit is permissible. Lastly, teachers do have the right to choose which regions, outside of the home region, are studied, giving them a considerable power to determine the issues which might be shared with children.

Many of the reservations about this geography curriculum are like those which have been made about other curriculum prescriptions, such as that for mathematics (Dowling and Noss, 1990), or for history. So, there is unease about the way in which the National Curriculum divides knowledge – geography, science or whatever – into ten levels of attainment; about the validity of the statements of attainment (ATs); about the ordering of the statements; and about the business of assessing children against the statements and then publicly reporting the results.

In geography the peculiar idea that children working towards level 5 should study a European Community country, unlike their classmates working towards level 4 has also been seen as an impracticable device which will cause substantial teaching and assessment problems. This is compared to the history curriculum (DES, 1991c) in which the ATs are content-free and where primary schools can tackle the content in any order, a necessary practical concession to small schools with mixed-age classes.

So, the English National Curriculum described history and geography in separate subject terms but in other countries, geography is generally organised within some kind of integrated curriculum arrangement – the social studies in the USA, Canada and New Zealand, topic work in England (until recently) and environmental studies in Scotland. Indeed, at the time of writing, there is a good chance that the English government may change its mind and demand a much more integrated primary curriculum. It will be seen that there are fears that within an integrated framework geography gets smothered by other concerns, and there is debate about whether social studies should be deconstructed, leaving history and geography as separate subjects.

The Scottish proposals had more affinity with American thinking than with the detailed prescriptions of the English curriculum. Yet, although the curriculum was organised under an integrated heading – environmental studies – the differences between it and the English proposals were not as great as might be imagined.

There were seven proposed Attainment Outcomes (AOs), comprising four content AOs (Science in the environment; Place, time and society; Living with technology; Healthy and safe living): two skills AOs (Investigating; Designing and making); and one attitudinal AO (Attitudes to the environment). The skills and attitudes AOs provided a basis for integration around process (see Chapter 9), but the other four were much less coherent.

The Place, time and society AO, for example, had eleven strands, three from geography – People and place, Journeys and movement, and Understanding maps; four from history – People in time, People and change, Cause and effect, and People and heritage; and four citizenship strands – Needs and society, Rights and responsibilities, Decision making and rules, and Conflict and its resolution. These eleven were pushed together by a general parochial and nationalistic choice of content, for the (hardly) 'expanding horizons' approach pervaded the proposals. Yet there was still much for teachers to do in order to make an integrated curriculum out of these eleven strands – which, it must be re-called, comprised one of seven AOs. Furthermore, the advice on content choice for these four AOs ran to eighteen separate points, and it is far from clear how many topics or mini-topics would have to be covered in order to meet satisfactorily the design criteria. The proposals said that

> teachers should bear in mind the importance of giving pupils the opportunity of pursuing a line of enquiry, without concern for 'subject' or other boundaries ... the 'general topic', which is likely to draw on several attainment outcomes should feature prominently in primary school programmes (Scottish Office, 1992, p.68).

However, difficulties could easily be seen in organising topics which blended the disparate elements which had coagulated to form 'environmental studies', while also meeting the design criteria and avoiding the pitfalls of superficial integration. It was far from obvious that geography would be better served by this form of integration at the planning level than it was by the English disintegration.

Even where geography has been clearly and simply delineated, problems still ensue. In 1984 the National Council for Geographic Education (NCGE) and the Association of American Geographers (AAG) identified five themes central to the study of geography, namely:

● Location – both in absolute terms (where a place is) and where places are relative to each other;
● Place – the physical and human characteristics of a place;
● Relationships within places – 'why things are like they are in a specific place' (Pigozzi, 1990, p.8);
● Movement – which includes the movement of ideas, materials and people, now and in the past;
● Regions – that is the study of complete spatial systems.

This list is open to criticism on the grounds that the order of the five themes could be seen as perpetuating 'a view of Geography as the archetypical source of trivia' (Pigozzi, 1990, p.12), at the expense of the belief that 'geography is more than location and more than a description: it is a perspective from which real-world problems may be assessed and solved' (*ibid*, p.9).

Thornton and Wenger (1990) noted that this programme had been advocated from time to time over the past century. As Muessig (1987) put it, writing of geography education in the USA,

> the history of geography instruction in the elementary school from its meager beginnings following the Revolution to the present day is unusual. Certain ideas tend to recur in cycles and methods of treatment over a century old are regarded as innovations when they reappear.

In the light of this history, any hope that wide-ranging plans for geography curricula will necessarily lead to wide-ranging classroom practices should be prudently modest: to date there is little evidence that the NCGE/AAG initiative has profoundly affected elementary geography teaching in the USA.

However plans turn out, they usually come with claims attached about what children will gain by following this or that 'six-year plan'. What is the value of school geography?

In part, of course, the answer depends upon the curriculum plan which they are following, and it depends even more on what the teacher actually delivers. Walford (1981), for example, argued that teachers' differing views of the *purpose* of geography in the curriculum could lead to them delivering very different curricula. One set of teachers might see geography within a general attempt to shape the society of the future, while another might see geography as a rather unimportant thing which children might encounter as a part of their general, child-centred, interest-driven educational programme. For others, maximising children's scores would be the priority, while a fourth set would work to produce 'little geographers'. These orientations can affect the delivery of any planned curriculum, and have done so, although it is arguable that guidelines such as the English geography curriculum simply represent a compilation of perspectives, which is fitting for geography as a synthesising subject but which gives teachers enormous scope to produce their own interpretations, either deliberately or by default, as they play up or avoid certain aspects. In the next chapter it will be shown that what is delivered in primary school geography has often been a scrawny caricature of the plans such as the NCGE's and the English National Curriculum.

## Summary

This review of the subject and of its definition for school consumption leads to five conclusions.

- Geography is a wide field of study, a feat of curriculum integration in itself.
- Geography is necessarily concerned with location, much as history is necessarily concerned with time, but geography is no more *about* location than history is about time.
- Geography should depend on the analysis and explanation of interactions within human societies, always from the distinctive perspective of an interest in the spatial features of those interactions. It should exercise the so-called 'higher-order' abilities as it addresses the question 'why?'.
- It is necessarily about human cultures and human values.
- There are disagreements about whether geography is best organised as a single field of study, or whether it is best taught as part of an integrated programme. The Scottish proposals suggest that it is not sufficient to judge this question on the basis of the planned curriculum: what matters is what children experience.

*Chapter 6*

# Primary School Geography

## What is taught and how

In this section we shall concentrate on international findings about what
children experience.

### Neglect

A surprising thing about primary school geography is that it is little
researched. While we may all have our own ideas about how it is taught
– and learned – there is remarkably little that can be done to establish
whether these views really do have much grounding in common
experience, or whether they are a reflection of our own particular
schemata and experience. In other words, the research perspective,
which is so useful for informing planning and pedagogy, is essentially
absent.

A recent work on the development of the American curriculum
contains two chapters on the emergence of the history curriculum but
none on the geographical elements of social studies (Popkewitz, 1987).
The *British Education Index* (BEI) lists articles in education periodicals.
In the years 1986–91 239 pieces were indexed under 'geography
education'. I estimated that only some 10 per cent of these articles were
research-based, as opposed to articles which put a case for some aspect
of geography education, or which reported on work done in the
classroom. Perhaps three of these pieces described what investigation
had shown children to be able to do. Mapping was the focus, which is
consistent with American data. ERIC is a computer data-base of mainly
American articles and papers. As with BEI, research papers do not

predominate. In 1992 25,841 items were listed under 'elementary education'. A search for geography-related pieces under 'elementary education' and related headings yielded 176 references, 37 per cent of which contained a reference to mapping. ERIC had 3,564 references to elementary phase mathematics, 3,999 to science and 5,576 to English and reading.

Primary geography is under-reported and under-researched. The largest single category of research into geography education is related to maps.

Such research as there is confirms that on both sides of the Atlantic (and of the Pacific too), geography has only been given passing attention (Thornton, 1988; Haas, 1989; DES, 1989a), subordinate to other aspects of the topics being studied, with the results that children know little factual geographical information and are deficient in their understanding of geographical concepts in general. Gritzner (1982, p.237) referred to

> the rather dismal status of [American] geographic instruction and training in the elementary and secondary schools. At the elementary levels such 'geography' as is taught often loses meaning and identity in the mish-mash known as the social studies (where geography may involve little more than a picture of the map of the world).

This should be seen against a background of threats to social studies in the USA – Joyce and colleagues (1991) reported research suggesting that, 'one trend regarding the scope of social studies is its deemphasis or omission from the curriculum in the lower elementary grades' (p.324). Given 'consistent findings over the years that students from elementary through high school find social studies to be one of the least interesting [American] school subjects' (Shaver, 1987, p.126), perhaps this is no bad thing.

*Localism*

The combination of the 'quantitative revolution' in geography and the misunderstanding of Piaget's writings combined to direct most geographical work into one channel, that of local studies. In the mistaken belief that nothing could be more concrete than the locality, local studies proliferated. Environmental issues might be raised, but these were local environmental issues, so the side of geography which deals with humans interacting with environments was sapped. Rather than measure the world, children mapped and surveyed the neighbourhood, charting the networks of sewers, shops, services and street furniture.

Known in the USA as the 'expanding horizons' curriculum, it generally involved the study of school, home and self in kindergarten, and then families and neighbourhoods in Years 1 and 2. Communities and cities in Y3 gave way to state history in Y4 and USA history in Y5. World cultures occupied Y6 (Manson, 1981). A similar pattern can be seen in Canada (Clarke *et al*, 1990) and New Zealand, is proposed for Scotland, and for France is commended by Marbeau (1988). Pigozzi's trenchant comment was that 'only a very small, and usually trivial, part of geography is currently taught in American elementary schools' (1990, abstract). The English evidence agrees (DES, 1978; 1989a).

A prominent feature has been map work, which is consistent with geography's claim to have a special contribution to make in the area of graphicacy. However, there are few reports of children learning to show the relative relationship between places in terms of, say, travelling times or ease and, although 'cognitive maps' have become fashionable, it is hard to find reports that anything much is done with them. Similar comments could be made about graphicacy in general, with the pervasive bar chart and the occasional (computer-produced) pie chart substituting for the whole range of graphical modes of displaying information. Interpreting graphical data also appears to be uncommon in the primary years.

Given the narrow horizons of primary geography, it is hardly surprising to find reports of 'geographical illiteracy': 'the overriding fact is that American students have not demonstrated basic competence along any dimensions of geographic learning' (Manson, 1981, p.247).

*Wider horizons*

There are, however, reports of curricula which do not conform to the expanding horizons or local studies mould (Fisher and Hicks, 1985) and some accounts of other teaching and learning approaches. In some schools local work involves decision-making – about where to put a new piece of furniture in a classroom, or about the renovation of a part of the school land; surveys typically play a part here, associated with discussion about what the costs and benefits would be of various options, and about why people act as they do (how do different weather conditions affect traffic flow past the school? Why?); simulations, computer-assisted learning and educational games are also sometimes used; local studies can be used to focus attention on global issues, not simply for the purpose of making contrasts, but also to identify similarities between *here* and *there*. Indeed, the Royal Geographical Society argued in 1950 (RGS, 1950/1976) that it was precisely this interplay of the local, national and global which distinguished geography from the dreaded social studies. Yet, despite the evidence of some diversity, the story is dominated by reports of teacher recitations.

## Teaching and learning methods

Most of the evidence about teaching methods says that a limited range was used. A study of eight English primary schools noted that the more formal methods of teaching geography prevailed over more active methods, such as simulations and games (Williams and Howley, 1989). In the USA, Shaver (1987) reported that low-level memorisation and comprehension activities were dominant in primary geography, while there is substantial agreement that teacher-led lessons, or recitations, have dominated social studies work in general (Cuban, 1991; Wilen and White, 1991). Associated with this was the influence of text books of indifferent qualities (Beck *et al*, 1989; Brophy *et al*, 1991).

There are considerable advantages for the teacher in recitation-style lessons: 'Teachers can diagnose students' comprehension of the content, control the topic through questioning and control students' behavior more easily through the question-answer format' (Wilen and White, 1991, p.485).

It also looks like 'real work' to the children (unlike discussions and simulations), leaves them clear about what they have to do in order to please the teacher, and is organisationally manageable. It can also be interesting (Knight, 1991a; Thornton, 1991). This is consistent with reports that teachers and student teachers draw on *general* educational ideas when doing social studies, rather than upon a subject-specific pedagogy. Teachers do vary their teaching according to the sort of activities which they see as sustainable in a subject context but the problem is that, especially in areas where their epistemology is naive and their view of what constitute suitable activities is deficient, they will tend to cope by devising activities by reference to general educational routines and principles, not from domain-specific insights.

Children, of course, come to school with existing, extensive private geographies (Bale, 1987), with a variety of schemata which will shape what they get from the recitations. Thornton and Wenger (1990) argued that the priority with this type of lesson is often content coverage, and that helping children to make connections, explore problems and understand the subject matter are neglected. We have already seen that such activities are thought to be important for effective learning in value-laden subjects. Quite simply, it is hard to see how these methods will help children to locate information, synthesise it, judge, defend their ideas, consider values and such like. Even proponents of direct instruction, such as recitations, accepted that the method is most suited to the mastery of factual material (Rosenshine, 1983). Other goals may best be served by less direct methods (Peterson, 1979).

*Assessment*

Characterised by their low status, humanities topics have been given little time, and taught in ways which could be identified with child-centred ideologies, but which could also be described as short on progression, coherence and continuity, lacking match with children's previous achievements, and indifferently assessed and evaluated. Effort, presentation, length and, sometimes, orthography, seem to have been important criteria in assessing children's geography, while evaluation often depended upon some guesstimate of how interested children had been. Williams and Howley (1989) found the schemes of work in nine primary schools to be silent on assessment in geography. It remains to be seen how far the English National Curriculum, which requires that teachers assess children throughout their schooling, reporting their achievements at ages seven and eleven, will change past practice.

American evidence suggests that prediction is not simple. Although the 1980s saw a growth of 'high status' (Kurfman, 1991) testing, that is testing in the 'basics', geography remained an area for 'low status' testing. The results made little impact on curriculum or pedagogy. Formative assessment, using data to tune learning to the learner, was rare (Thornton and Wenger, 1990): diagnostic assessment (to identify the cause of geography learning problems) rarer (Kurfman, 1991). Since the tests appear to have been fact-driven (Thornton and Wenger, 1990), 'checkup tests and quizzes', often 'glib, trite, decontextualised common-sense, civic-type questions' (Nickell, 1992, pp.92–3), embracing the sort of locational trivia which Pigozzi excoriated, perhaps it was fortunate that the results were neglected. However, HMI, visiting New York schools, expressed general unease about the impact of testing on teaching,

> rather than providing an enabling framework for teachers to exercise their
> professional judgement in deciding the best patterns of organisation to
> meet individual needs, the objectives lead, although by no means
> invariably, to fragmented and itemised teaching and approaches: in effect,
> to deskilling teachers  (DES, 1990b, p.22).

It is not clear how the English National Curriculum arrangements
differ.

## Summary

The international evidence is overwhelming.  The geography which is
taught in primary schools is a shadow of the geography intended for
them and of the academic field of study.  The consistency with which
this is found should make one cautious about believing that the English
curriculum will break the mould.

## Why was geography taught like this?

### Classrooms

A powerful reason for believing that planned curriculum change will
hardly affect practice is that widespread practices may reflect common,
dominating structural factors at work.

> Why has the core pattern of teaching practice endured over most of the
> 20th century? ... in view of the changes that have occurred in the
> occupation of teaching since the early 1900s and the advice that
> researchers and policy makers have given to social studies teachers to
> improve practice, why has there been a pervasive consistency in teaching
> practices – what many have labeled a *limited repertoire* (Cuban, 1991,
> p.205).

One line of explanation has already been noticed in the discussion of
the prevalence of this 'core pattern' of recitation:  classrooms almost
have a life of their own.  Teachers need to establish routines, minimise
ambiguity, assume that children have similar levels of understanding,
dominate proceedings, ask plenty of questions, all because this makes

their complex job manageable. However, teaching about values, which is a part of geography work, implies the use of methods in which the teacher has to 'let go', to abandon the position of a didact in authority, and to take risks. Galton and Williamson (1992) have shown how hard teachers find this and how, as a result, children have reason to like activities which are clearly defined and readily performed. Work which threatens the smooth running of the class is avoided or re-conceived – by both pupils and teachers – into a routinised form, often at the expense of the very lessons which that particular pedagogy was intended to teach. In mathematics, for example, discussion, exploration and practical work are all liable to be replaced by less risky alternatives which compromise the message of mathematics as a practical, problem-working form of enquiry and understanding (Desforges and Cockburn, 1987). Johnston (1988) has shown the difficulties attached to constructivist approaches to science teaching, echoing Olson's point (1980) about the way that high school science teachers recast an investigative science project to make it easier for them to manage. Parsons (1986) developed a similar thesis with respect to the English high school 'Geography for the Young School Leaver' project. In the words of Doyle and Ponder (1977/8) a 'practicality ethic' works as a disincentive to risk-taking; and working on values and controversies is risk-taking.

In this way it is possible to understand Thornton's (1992) skilful social studies teachers, Mrs Nelson, for one:

> This was not a classroom where either voices were raised or harsh glances exchanged ... the lesson proceeded smoothly ... routines were in place ... the students seldom had to be reminded ... With only minor exceptions, students were on task throughout the 30-minute lesson (p.85).

'Was this a good curriculum?', he asked, concluding that it fell far short of the ideals of the National Council for Geographical Education. There seems to be a tendency for classrooms to take on this traditional shape.

It is important to ask whether there have been changes *within* the recitation pattern over this century, for changes to a form may be as significant as a change from one form of teaching to another. Furthermore, there is a danger of excessive determinism, of casting teachers in the role of unwitting dupes who imagine they have free will when they do not. Despite these important qualifications, the prevalence of long-established forms of geography schooling is a significant reminder of the limits to the power of change in education.

## Teachers' general educational beliefs

Teachers' general beliefs about education, particularly their curricular beliefs (about *what* children should learn) and their psychological beliefs (about what children *can* do) help us to understand the nature of geography teaching.

Alexander (1984; 1992a) was critical of the child-centred beliefs which teachers acquired, principally, he contended, through initial teacher education. His criticism was not so much that it is wrong to consider the child when planning a curriculum, but rather that the curriculum should be a mediation between the academic subject (geography, in this case) and the epistemic subject (the child). Hitherto teachers have often claimed to be teachers of the 'whole child' and rejected as the inappropriate imposition of secondary school ways of working claims that they should be teaching academic subjects, with the exception of maths and English. This has suffered somewhat in the face of the enforced introduction of national curricula in Wales, Scotland, England and Northern Ireland, although I doubt that we have seen the last of the belief that teaching children, not teaching subjects, is the job of primary schools. Alexander's claim is that it militates against systematic and informed teaching, not least against informed teaching of marginal subjects such as geography.

## Teachers' knowledge of geography

Teachers generally know little geography, and are over-reliant on their own naive schemata. Their general educational beliefs can discourage thought about geographical education and they may be uneasy about tackling the controversial issues which geography carries with it.

As we have seen (Chapter 4), the view which one has of a subject is likely to be related to the way in which one teaches. Important though it is that people who are going to teach geography know some geographical information, it is also vital that they understand what sort of subject it is, what its coverage, principles, procedures and problems are. The evidence is that initial teacher education courses have little geographical content and that student teachers' ideas about social studies education have been based mainly on their general educational thinking, rather than derived from any understanding of the social studies (Adler, 1984). In Williams and Howley's eight primary schools (1989), seven out of the seventy teachers had some geography qualification and only one had attended any geography-oriented in-service activity in the previous three years. Even teachers who were identified as skilled American geography teachers lacked much grasp of modern geography (Thornton and Wenger, 1990), while the report that 48 per cent of English teachers surveyed in 1989 felt competent in geography and that only 2 per cent thought they needed substantial in-service help (Wragg *et al*, 1989), flies in the face of evidence of prevalent poor practice and raises the thought that a major problem could be that teachers don't know what they don't know.

Teachers' educational beliefs about geography may well reflect some unease about its suitability for younger children, particularly when it moves away from study of the concrete locality. Much of the research published in the late 1960s and 1970s, emphasising as it did the weaknesses of primary children's reasoning (Rhys, 1972), allowed the conclusion to be drawn that the subject (caricatured as abstract, adult and remote) was essentially unsuited to primary school children. More recent research has pointed out that there is much of value that children *can* achieve but older beliefs survive and can act as deterrents to geography work in the primary school.

Besides the issue of subject matter knowledge, there are important questions concerning teachers' technical competence. A re-examination of the example of controversial issues demonstrates an extreme case of this.

Geography, according to many commentators, is about controversial issues, although the English government attempted to amputate that concern, leaving the subject as a body of facts and techniques with no-where to go. This echoes reports that teachers, too, were chary of controversial issues (Storm, 1970; Marsh, 1987; Shaver, 1987). At least four explanations of this may be advanced. The first is that teachers work in settings which discourage the investigation of certain values, and that they are, in any case, disinclined to do so because of their own socialisation and roles. The second is that they eschew such issues because they doubt the efficacy of tackling them through school. There is certainly a lot of evidence that the effects of values education can be fleeting, slight and uneven (e.g. Milner, 1983; Shaver, 1987). Thirdly, there may be at work a view of childhood as an age of innocence, in which such issues are seen as inappropriate for primary school children. Fourthly, it is not easy to teach controversial issues, for it is not enough to just present information on the topic, as Woff argued,

> as so often in teaching, the content cannot be relied upon to have the
> desired effect on the learner – there is a need for issues to be highlighted
> and discussed *in the context of an appropriate pedagogy* (1991, p.33:
> emphasis added).

Porter (1991) identified a number of techniques which are appropriate
to teaching about controversial issues (see also Fisher and Hicks, 1985),
which raises the question of whether these techniques are taught to
teachers. The evidence of research into the way teachers learn about
geography, history and the social studies in general (Adler, 1984)
suggests that they are not helped towards a pedagogy for handling
values and controversy. It is scarcely surprising, then, if such issues are
ignored in many primary classrooms.

*Subject integration*

It may seem paradoxical that a book on subject integration should
identify integration as a reason for indifferent geography teaching. The
argument will be developed that the idea of subject integration is a
powerful one, but its realisation has been puny.

Integrated approaches to the humanities/social studies have been
normal in the USA, Canada, New Zealand and Australia, and
commonplace in the UK (Tann, 1987). A particular difficulty with this
approach is that geography and history fare badly, with their distinctive
range of concerns being washed out by the bleach of subject integration.

> The weakest work in primary schools occurs when too many aspects of
> different subjects are roped together within integrated themes or topic
> work ... The most serious casualties of this practice are history and
> geography. They are often not well taught and are under-represented in
> many primary schools (HMI, 1990, pp.6–7).

Elsewhere in the same report it is averred that 'history and geography
hardly exist in practice in many primary schools' (p.1). Later it will be
argued that this is not a necessary consequence of integration, yet it is
clearly a common enough consequence to permit the comment that
where teachers are wedded to integrated, topic and project approaches,
the teaching of geography has often suffered for their beliefs.

*Resources*

In mathematics there exist a number of packages which support individualised work, which is taken by the student at her pace. While there are doubts about whether this is the best way of developing mathematical concepts and of encouraging children to apply maths to practical problem solving (Desforges and Cockburn, 1987), there is no doubt that suitable materials support certain ways of working. There is little by way of information on the type of geography resources in English schools, let alone about their use. However, the American evidence is that textbooks set the curriculum (Shaver, 1987; Brophy, 1992). Marsh (1987), reporting on a project to develop a social studies curriculum in Australia, said that teachers tended to treat the teachers' handbook as a bible. In the USA, social studies texts tend to promote the more 'closed', factual side of geography (Beck *et al*, 1989; Thornton and Wenger, 1990; Brophy *et al*, 1991). Bearing in mind that publishers will produce what the market will buy, we might predict that texts will tend to address the lowest common denominator, avoiding 'marginal' topics and 'impractical' activities.

Ironically, it is the local emphasis in geography which means that resources can only explain a part of teaching practices, since texts cannot tell teachers how to do geography in *this* locality. In geography as it has often been practised, teachers have been thrown upon their own resources. It is only with the coming of a curriculum which requires all schools to study certain non-local themes that the possibility arises in England of geography texts having much influence on primary practice. In the USA there has been something of a *de facto* national curriculum, which has permitted researchers to examine the way in which geography texts support children's learning.

A study by Haas (1988) suggests that these are not idle concerns. Analysing the geographical concepts contained in 20 American grade 1–4 social studies books from five publishers, she concluded that physical geography was over-represented, and noted that of the NCGE/AAG's five themes, location, region and relations within places were under-represented. Not only was there an emphasis on the facts of geography, but also those concepts that were introduced were not re-visited, applied and extended.

> Nor do the texts require students to do much of the critical thinking required to form rules and solve problems. Instead, the textbook publishers have selected a method of presentation that encourages the

learning of isolated facts which are quickly forgotten (p.17).

Work by Beck *et al* (1989), Brophy *et al* (1991) and Brophy (1992) has confirmed that American texts handle geography themes in ways which are unlikely to foster understanding and the generation of networks of meaning, much less problem-working, critical thinking and decision-making.

That is not to deny that teachers can and do modify texts, use them as stimulus, and generally build upon them. Unfortunately, there is a strong suspicion that the texts are not always 'improved' in ways which are educationally effective. Milburn (1972) showed that children in Year 3 were able to define correctly only 8.8 per cent of the 47 geography concepts which were appropriate to their age, while Year 6 children did better but still only succeeded with 29.7 per cent of the 215 concepts used. There are problems with his research methods which may have led to an under-estimate of children's understanding, but even so it is obvious that concepts covered in books and in class are not well understood by primary children. He identified three sets of concept which needed to be treated with particular care:

● Commonplace concepts – island ('a little kind of box in the middle of the road'), river ('a dug ditch'), valley ('a little village') – where teachers might assume an understanding which, in fact, children often lack.
● Homonyms – cape ( a garment), relief (thank goodness!).
● Homophones – moor (more), irrigation (immigration).

Uncertainty whether schools will ever wish to spend a fair proportion of their funds on geography resources may – or may not – be cause for re-assurance.

*Time*

Thrown upon their own resources for geography, teachers say that they lack the time to take the initiative and go beyond the obvious. Time is not an absolute concept but a relative one, and the complaint that there is too little time to work out good geography practice is best seen as a statement about priorities. The literature agrees that geography has had a low priority in teachers' thinking (Alexander, 1984; Thornton and Wenger, 1990). This is an extension of the way that social studies or the humanities are generally regarded. Writing of the USA, Shaver (1987) noted reports that between 60 and 90 minutes a week was spent on primary social studies, unless assemblies or other special events intruded. In France, a more generous 2 hours a week for geography and history is allocated in Y4–6 (DES, 1991d), but in New Zealand and in Australia a lesser priority is given to social studies (Simon, 1992; Marsh, 1987). Marbeau (1988) remarked that in the late 1970s teachers in France were unable to benefit from in-service training on the humanities because up-dating the French and mathematics curricula took priority.

It is not necessarily the case that the amount of time spent learning something is related to achievement, and the research into 'time on task' has produced contradictory results. The significance of the small amount of time spent on geography is not that there is a direct relationship with children's learning, but more that it signifies a field of study which is hardly important enough to take pains over. Related to this is the belief that if effective geography and history work need to have some depth, then it follows that either more time must be found for the humanities, or that the routinised, didactic methods of teaching will prevail. The irony is that if these methods prevail then the geography process attainment target (AT1) will be stunted, with the result that the content is unlikely to be understood, remaining inert and learned by rote (see Chapter 3 above). Later it will be argued that subject integration offers the only plausible way out of this conflict between the practicality ethic and the ambitious demands of modern geography curricula.

This discussion of the reasons why primary geography has so often been taught in certain, common ways has emphasised factors which constrain the teacher. They do not, however, compel the teacher. Furthermore, even when circumstances lead teachers to follow certain methods, it is important to remember that there is enormous room for variation *within those methods*. For example, expository teaching is not necessarily dull, nor necessarily bad. It is, however, just one way of teaching geography. It is now appropriate to turn to what else may be done in the geography curriculum.

## Harbingers of better practice

In this section I discuss three factors related to the enhancement of school geography.

## A *system*

A necessary condition for system-wide development is a system-wide requirement that geography is taught, combined with some form of specification of what is to be taught, particularly in terms of the concepts and abilities which should be fostered. This cannot guarantee that geography teaching will not tend to be a reduced version of the curriculum vision, since implementation invariably changes planned innovations.

> faithful implementation is sometimes undesirable (because the idea is bad), sometimes impossible (because power won't permit), and often unforeseeable (because it depends on what people bring to it as well as what's in it) (Fullan, 1991, p.93).

Even in the coercive English National Curriculum it is still worth remembering Fullan's injunction, 'do not expect all or even most people to change' (*ibid*, p.106). However, some system-wide requirements are necessary, for without them there is very little to counteract those forces which have led to the scene described in earlier sections.

It is easy to envisage a number of forms which these requirements might take. In England the curriculum is specified in detail, both in terms of the content to be covered and in terms of concepts and abilities to be fostered. Recognising that teachers have considerable scope for subverting prescriptions of this sort, the government has made sure that achievement norms are specified for ages 7 and 11. These norms are the level 2 and the level 4 statements, which stipulate, for example, that at level 2 children should,

> demonstrate an understanding that most homes are part of a settlement, and that settlements vary in size. Give reasons why people make journeys of different lengths. Identify how goods and services needed in the local community are provided (DES, 1991b, p.19).

The level 4 norms for this AT, Human Geography are,

> explain why few people live in some areas and many people live in others. Describe the layout and function of a small settlement or part of a large settlement. Explain the impact of recent or current changes [in that settlement]. Explain why roads and railways may not always take the shortest route between the places they link. Give reasons for the ways in which land is used, how conflict can arise because of competition over the

use of land, and for the location of different types of economic activity (*ibid*, p.20).

Teachers are obliged to assess children's geographical understanding against these norms as a regular part of their classroom activity. What gives the curriculum requirements force is not the time-honoured system of inspection (which in England has recently been transformed), nor the way teachers are more accountable to boards of school governors for their professional activities, but the fact that children's achievements, measured against these norms, have to be reported to parents and are published in an aggregated form so that schools are to be compared on the basis of children's achievements in the National Curriculum. It is important that schools are seen to do well in the resulting league tables because parents have some choice of the school their child is to attend and schools' funding is directly dependent on the number of children who enrol.

There are indeed, many grounds for unease about the English model, as we have seen. The system is new, and because it is far from certain that geography is regarded in the same light as the 'core' subjects of maths, science and English, it is doubtful whether compliance with the National Curriculum goes far beyond tokenism. The assessment arrangements may not have the force in geography that they have in the core subjects (schools will not be compelled to submit children to national testing), with the result that there is less reason for schools to stick to the broad aims embodied in the curriculum. In particular, there are fears that, as in maths and English, the more obvious, simple and routine aspects of the subject will, in practice, predominate with the result that geography will remain essentially mapping and local studies. At the end of 1992 a review of the operation of the just-established National Curriculum seemed likely to lead to a down-grading of the humanities to provide more time for 'getting down to basics'. Yet because geography has been so badly served by the curricula of the past, then even partial compliance with the new national systems can be seen as an enormous improvement. Initially there will be problems in conforming to these systems, but once the National Curriculum requirements have become familiar and have been built in to initial teacher education programmes, then change will accelerate.

*Resources*

As American publishers have demonstrated, the existence of a common curriculum, either in the strong form of the English National Curriculum, or in the weak form of mandatory guidelines for school action, provides an incentive for resource production. It may be hoped that better resources will be developed in response to new curricula and new markets, although the fact that it is for schools to decide which places they study will mean that publishers face a less certain market for geography books than for history ones, since history topics are, mainly, prescribed. There is anecdotal evidence that teachers prefer the history approach and the resources which accompany it.

The hope may be pious, not least because, as Apple has argued (1986), in order to maximise profits, publishers need to give teachers what they want, which may not be what the curriculum needs. It is easy to see how publishers may reject proposals which do not envisage the standard 'double page spread' layout that can trivialise all before it; or geography books which are to be read as 'thick descriptions'; or works containing tasks which may require thought and disrupt classrooms; which use the Peters projection and/or do not put the Atlantic Ocean in the centre (in the case of European books), or place the Pacific at the centre (in books for Pacific pupils).

Yet, research into school texts has flourished in the USA over the past dozen years, and if poor books are produced, it is not for want of knowledge about the characteristics of those which promote meaningful learning. The problem is more of a marketing problem than a research problem.

*The 'basics'*

This raises a theme to be developed in Chapters 9 and 10, namely that geography (and history or the social studies) are important in themselves but that they are most likely to attract serious support if they become seen as areas which are fundamentally important to the development of children's language abilities. The history of the past two decades has been marked by continuous concern about 'the basics', defined as maths, English (French in France) and science. We have already noted that the priority given to the basics has worked against the humanities, and even where there is a strong requirement that the humanities are taught, as there is in England, it has been suggested that the same squeeze might become yet more pressing. Yet there is very little that is basic about the basics. Once the rudiments of reading and writing have been grasped, progress is to a greater (English) or lesser (mathematics) extent through application – through reading for a purpose, writing for an audience, applying mathematics to a problem, or working scientifically to tease out the best way of doing something. The social studies can deliver all of this: indeed, they must do so if children are to work towards the bold claims made for school geography, for example. If geography can be seen to be a powerful agent for the development of the basics, it would not justify geography's place in the curriculum, but given that geography is in the curriculum on other grounds, it constitutes a powerful case for investing seriously in quality geography work. *Pari passu* for the social studies in general.

## Research and techniques

Given a context which is broadly – albeit weakly – supportive of school geography, what might be attained?

The rest of this chapter surveys research findings. Some of this research was done in the context of social studies generally but it is included where there is reason to believe that it is as applicable to geography as to civics or to history.

### Maps

Maps are systematic ways of describing features of space.

Three points need to be insisted upon here. One is that the systematic nature of maps means that there are certain regularities and known elements to them which mean that it is relatively easy to write behavioural objectives *and* to organise them into a hierarchy or taxonomy. So, a basal idea is that maps are plan views; some grasp of directions and symbols follows; and then co-ordinates and perhaps contours; and then with the notion of scale proving rather more difficult. This taxonomy can be rendered into fairly tight objectives, since it describes a well-defined and closed system. It is hardly surprising, then, that so much work has been done on children's mapping abilities.

Maps, it must remembered, are ways of describing geographical features and abstractions. However convenient they are, they are not geography, any more than history is time: maps are not the essence of geography.

This leads to the third point, which is that maps come not just in many scales, and on various projections, but in many forms too. The variations in scale are familiar, although there is evidence that children, and some adults too, find scale to be one of the hardest things about maps to grapple with. The problem of projection can be illustrated by peeling a (roundish) orange and trying to flatten out the skin, but it is hopeful to expect that children will be too sure about the relative merits, say, of Peters and Mercator projections.

Apart from variations in portrayal and scale, there are also maps which show the distribution in 'real space' of various phenomena of interest to geographers, such as the incidence of two-car families in a region, or of water pollution, or of areas partitioned according to the number of days in which the mean temperature is below zero, or of cases of poverty-related illnesses. These maps, effective ways of presenting evidence of the variety of lived experience over space, receive rather less attention in schools than their importance merits. Another sort of map does not claim to depict 'real space', but shows the subjectivity of space, charting, for example, the journey times from one centre to a variety of others, or showing routes and connections, as does the map of the London Underground. Subjective maps have been a fruitful research topic for those interested in children's development because it tells us something about ways in which children typically understand space (which may be useful information for teachers and curriculum makers), and it also shows how information is perceived, represented and stored (which is of interest to developmental psychologists).

Reviewing the research, Boardman (1989) said that children enter school with a sense of place, the nature of which relates to their experiences. As children pass the age of nine a gender-related difference in these experiences becomes apparent, with boys engaging in outdoor play which takes them further afield than girls. Their maps reflect this (Matthews, 1984), so that at age eight the ratio of the standard distance shown on girls' maps compared to boys was reported as 1:1.02 (that is to say that boys mapped a slightly greater area than did girls). At the age of nine Matthews found a bigger difference, reporting a ratio of 1:1.68, which is close to findings from American research.

Differences have also been reported in the way that boys and girls represent space. There is a slight tendency for girls to add people to their maps and for boys to show means of transport. Girls give rather more detail, while boys use a broader brush to depict a bigger area.

Boys were better at getting spatial elements in their correct relationship to each other, and they also mastered the abstract conventions of mapping earlier than girls did (Matthews, 1984). This may be related to the finding that boys from the age of eight onwards show greater facility with spatial visualisation and orientation, not just in geography but in mathematics too. This raises the issue of the degree to which these differences in the way boys and girls represent the world are determined by their experiences as opposed to predispositions in their genetics. It is a theme to which we shall return.

Research into children's abilities with topological maps has shown that six year olds can appreciate the idea that a map is a plan view, and they can trace routes on aerial photographs and simple maps and identify some features with success (Blaut and Stea, 1971). In fact four year olds playing with cars on a mat which is marked out in a street pattern are doing the same thing, although it is unlikely that they are conscious of doing mapwork. Likewise, young children may also encounter 'maps' of Little Red Riding Hood's journey, or of the flight of the Three Little Pigs, and Blades and Spencer (1986) record that they can follow routes through plans of mazes and that children aged about five can be taught some uses of globes, models and compasses. Six year olds seem to have no problem in principle with the idea of map symbols and eight year olds can understand the idea of map orientation and act upon it when participating in treasure hunts (Boardman, 1989). These years, between age six and age eight were seen as years of considerable advance in map interpretation by Blaut and Stea. Interestingly, they found little evidence that children performed better with maps of familiar areas than with maps of unfamiliar areas.

Thereafter children's difficulties in interpreting maps are partly related to the way in which maps are designed, since many are so rich in information that not only is it hard for the child to be sure what they should look at, but it is also easy for them to get attracted by some of the welter of detail and to lose sight of the overall pattern (Bartz, 1970). This phenomenon is characteristic of the way in which novices, as opposed to experts, see things. Where the novice chess player is confronted with a chaos of pieces, the expert sees patterns and a range of possibilities. So too with maps. If children are to notice general features and patterns, they need to be guided – 'instructions have to be explicit, otherwise teacher and pupil will be looking at different things' (Graves, 1975, p.151). This leads to the optimistic conclusion that reported difficulties with map reading may resemble the reports of children's difficulties with historical time by being outcomes of indifferent teaching or of no systematic teaching about map use. This is emphatically not a call for children to be taught even more conventional map symbols but a claim that they should be guided in what to look for in maps and that they should be encouraged to develop some kind of metacognition – or active overview – of how some maps might be read.

A less optimistic conclusion is also necessary. Some things, like using atlases with their conventions of colouring and longitude and latitude, or coping with the issue of scale, or interpreting contours, let alone drawing cross-sections, are going to cause problems for most primary children. These are not simply problems caused by lack of practice, for they are also procedurally complex and conceptually abstract ideas. It makes sense in geography, as in history, to have a clear view of what sort of ideas about maps are to be developed; to make those ideas few rather than many; and to concentrate on them, rather than to proliferate points. There is also a case for introducing ideas in a concrete form – introducing the idea of orienting a map, for example, in the context of work on the school site – before developing the more abstract generalisation. In this spirit Boardman (1989) has commended forms of orienteering as ways of helping children to read maps and his review might usefully be read alongside Catling's list of 37 ways of developing five to eight year olds' understanding of maps and globes (1990b).

*Concept development*

Wrongly, it is sometimes assumed that concept development is a path from the absence of concepts to their correct formulation. Leaving aside the notion that concepts necessarily have a correct formulation, there is still a problem. Frequently, the learning problem is not so much the absence of a concept as the presence of a misconception, or alternative concept, which interferes with learning. Children have their own, private geographies before they come to learn formal geography. As we have already noticed (Milburn, 1972) children also have problems with homonyms and homophones and with geographical concepts such as cape, irrigation, ford and relief.

Furthermore, children who have a concept of 'Eskimos', living in igloos and fishing through holes in the ice are likely to find it tricky to form a concept of the Inuit living with the trappings of modern civilisation – both good and bad – in a tedious wilderness. The alternative concept interferes with the better concept. Camperell and

Knight (1991, p.572), considering children's reading strategies made a related observation, ' repeatedly, researchers have found that readers distort the meaning of a text to conform to pre-existing knowledge and are unaware of misinterpreting what they read'. It follows that it is essential for the teacher to be aware of this process of mis-interpretation and to have to hand strategies for limiting it. We have seen that these conceptual problems have not been well handled by the producers of classroom geography materials.

They have, however, been addressed in the context of science (Osborne and Freyberg, 1985; Knight, 1989a), where an important teaching activity consists of finding out what misconceptions children have and then planning ways of presenting them with evidence which may prompt them to accommodate their ideas to the new information by forming a better concept. Difficult in science (Johnston, 1988), and in general (Wittrock, 1986, p.309), this can be harder still in geography where forming a better concept may involve challenging children's values. Trying to abrade stereotypes about the Third World, poverty, women and technological progress is, to put it mildly, hard. But, it is harder still to see how effective geography work can take place unless these alternative concepts are recognised in the first place. Methods of identifying them include children completing a semantic differential exercise, in which they had to rate Nigeria, for example, on a number of scales which might include 'rich ... poor', 'peaceful ... violent', 'modern ... backward'. Alternatively, they might be given a list of adjectives and asked to pick those which applied to Nigeria, or, thirdly, they might be asked just to say anything which they knew or thought about the place. This probing, done before the topic is finally planned, gives the teacher material on which to base a strategy with which to attempt concept modification.

There is also the business of teaching concepts which are likely to be fresh to children. 'Contour' might be such a concept. Martorella (1991) has suggested a general concept teaching strategy which is presented in a modified form here:

1. identify examples of the concept (contour lines);
2. direct attention to the key features of contour lines;
3. examine examples of contour lines, referring back to their key features;
4. consider counter-examples (ie instances of 'contour' lines representing different heights but crossing; cases of 'contour' lines joining spot heights of different values);

5. use a child-friendly definition;
6. relate to other, relevant concepts (spot height, sea level);
7. practise and assess.

Point 6 is worth further comment. Isolated concepts will prove hard for the child to retrieve from mental storage and may easily become 'lost' to all intents and purposes. 'Understanding', claimed Entwistle, 'depends on being able to develop a web of interconnections which relate previous knowledge and experience to the new ideas being represented' (cit Ghaye and Robinson, 1987, p.129). As we saw in Chapter 4, activities need to be provided which encourage children to make links – and to rearrange links – amongst concepts. Ghaye and Robinson commend concept mapping, where children are encouraged to shuffle linked concepts, and to create hierarchies and connections.

Whatever other conclusions may be drawn from research into concept formation, one stands out. Simply defining concepts is of little value, leading at best to definitions being parroted into short-term memory. This raises important questions about glossaries and the treatment of concepts in general in school texts.

### Distant places

In a sense this simply continues the previous point, for learning about other places may be seen as a special case of concept formation. In Chapter 4 the view that children could only work on the immediate, physically concrete environment was rejected. However, unless the attempt is made to present other places in non-stereotypical terms, then stereotypes will, unsurprisingly, result. Plentiful examples of this may be seen by examining almost any 'European Studies' work, which seems doomed to perpetuate stereotypes about Lederhosen, pasta, baguettes and bull fights. That is not to say that work on distant places will be dull. I completely agree with Marsden (1991) that it should be vivid, visual, varied and venturesome, so that the children get a strong, vicarious experience of distant place.

Children's conceptions of other distant places and distant peoples have become a topic of considerable research interest.

Weigand (1991) examined the knowledge which seven and eleven year olds had of other countries in the days before the onset of the geography National Curriculum. He included places mentioned by at least 20 per cent of his sample – hardly a stiff test of children's awareness of other places.  Seven year olds showed awareness of the African continent, of America, India, Russia, China, Australia, France and Spain.  Their knowledge could be described as largely undifferentiated, an awareness of the existence of large land masses, but not of the variations within them.  Eleven year olds had a more extensive and differentiated knowledge, mentioning, for example, most West European countries.  Yet, interestingly, despite the revolutions taking place in Eastern Europe at the time, and the Israeli involvement in Lebanon, knowledge of these countries was scant, leading him to suggest that 'places which only appear on the news remain "unknown" to children' (p.146).

Weigand identified differences between schools in the knowledge which eleven year olds displayed of other countries, saying that 'the world map of children at Remote Estate Primary school [in an educational priority area] is the most restricted' (p.146).  Clearly, he concluded, for greatest effectiveness, teachers should try to build up a baseline, an account of the knowledge with which children start, an idea which we have met before in the context of concept development.

Milner (1983) approached the topic of distant places with a particular interest in the development of racism, stereotyping and prejudice, all of which are dispositions to which the humanities should be fundamentally inimical.  He reported that children from age three onwards showed racial awareness and that 10 per cent of English three year olds had negative attitudes to blacks, a figure which rose to 40 per cent of four year olds.  Between the ages of seven and nine, stereotyped attitudes crystallised, with prejudice intensifying thereafter.  Research into the effect of teaching on racial prejudice was reported to be somewhat equivocal, and some evidence was cited that prejudice could be increased by teaching.  The type of teaching may explain the response, for, as Milner put it,

> some West Indian dancing this week, some Indian cookery next, and a multi-faith assembly once a term does not amount to multicultural education;  and in this scheme of things, this month's project on Jamaica assumes the same weight as last month's project on dinosaurs, and somewhere along the line the point has been lost (1983, p.225).

At the heart of any worthwhile work on other cultures is the fundamental, absolutely pervasive notion that people are human, wherever they live, which means that they make what seem to them to be intelligent decisions about their interaction with space.  This premise is fundamental to geography and to history. Consequently, the lived environment has to be seen as the product of people's best choices, which means that school geography involves trying to understand those choices and their makers. Slater (1992) has suggested that a major development in geography in the next few years will be a growing emphasis on people–people relationships in space, rather than just on the objective facts about space. In the context of the study of distant places that not only implies that geography should be an attempt to understand why people *choose* to live as they do, but also that, following the World Studies projects, geography should involve thought about our relationships with different peoples in distant places.

Meck (1986) described a topic on native North Americans which was designed to counter stereotyping. It began with Y6 children saying, drawing and displaying what they knew, to begin with, about these peoples. A tape/slide sequence 'unlearning Indian stereotypes' was designed to show that these images were insulting, that Amerindians had been oppressed and that their cultures were diverse. Case studies of the Iroquois, the Navaho and the Hopi followed, in which comparisons were made between their lives then and now. The general themes of justice, diversity and stereotyping ran through this project. Although there is no compelling evidence of the project's effectiveness, I have described it to illustrate an approach which is commended in the literature on teaching about distant places – and times.

So, others' lives are not properly described by lists of *exotica*, although that will fascinate and flourish, but rather by attempts to notice the similarities between life *here* and *there*, to explain them and to *complicate* children's world view. In a real sense this is about generating better concepts in the place of worse, and the same teaching techniques may be applied. However, we cannot hope for too much: writing of school history, HMI said 'historical skills may not open closed minds; they may plant a nagging grain of doubt in them' (1985, p.32). The same is surely true of geography.

## Questioning

This has been a substantial research topic, probably because it is relatively easy for researchers to tally and analyse questions. Typically, the advice is that good teaching involves the use of plenty of questions and that good questioning involves plenty of open-ended judgement and reasoning questions (Dillon, 1982). In this way 'teachers can diagnose students' comprehension of the content, control the topic through questioning, and control students' behavior more easily through the question-answer format' (Wilen and White, 1991, p.485).

Research has blighted these assumptions. As Wilen and White's quotation hints, questioning may not be characterised by high-level questions – the opposite is generally reported, with questions in geography, as in other subjects, being usually closed and factual, intended to engage students, to control the less attentive and to sweep them all along towards the teacher's goal. In fact, this predominance of lower-level questions may be necessary as a way of calling to mind information which students need before most of them can respond fully to open-ended questions (D. Hargreaves, 1984), and it might actually be quite effective (Wilen and White, 1991). This interpretation leads us to see questioning as a way of getting audience participation in the teacher's recitation.

In Chapter 3 we noted the counter-view that teacher questioning does '*not* stimulate and might well depress the expression of student thought' (Dillon, 1982, p.146). It was observed that in the humanities it is important to make plenty of room for mental activity, of which student questions might be both a sign and a part. These, Dillon remarked 'enjoy a generous place in educational theory but a small one in classroom practice' (1988, p.8), students' questions being few in number and trivial in nature. We have already noted the importance of connecting geographical concepts with children's private geographies, and student questions offer an important way by which the knowledge generated in the classroom may be connected to the child's understandings.

Within a whole-class setting it is possible to encourage children to raise questions simply by making time for it and being prepared to wait and be patient. It can help to get literate children to jot down questions first and to compare notes with one another. It is obviously important to value the questions and to do this regularly. Group-work may offer a way of allowing more children to be actively engaged in making sense of geography and asking questions, but if ever there was an issue where it would be important for the teacher to be a sharp-minded enquirer into her own – and colleagues' – practices, this is it, given the practical problems and considerable doubts which have been described in Chapter 4.

*Group-work*

It will be recalled that there is some American evidence that groups can be made to work effectively (Slavin, 1990); that there is a body of psychological thought which regards group-work as a potentially powerful learning aid (Vygotsky, 1962; Perret-Clermont, 1980; Hahn, 1991); and that it is thought to be especially appropriate in humanities subjects where questions of value and of judgement are concerned (Peterson, 1979; Alleman and Rosaen, 1991). However, reports of properly designed and evaluated studies of collaborative learning in geography are scarce: Slavin (1990) listed two in his review of 60 reports: both showed that collaborative learning was productive in geography. Winitzky (1992) reported that working in pairs could be helpful to both partners, even where one was more able than the other.

However, there are reasons to be cautious in interpreting this research. As will be further demonstrated in Chapter 8, some of the collaborative learning techniques seem to have been most developed in the context of supporting pupil mastery of essentially factual, fixed material. Secondly, there is concern that in mixed sex groups the interaction can be male dominated. Thirdly, the 'Group Investigation' technique which is identified by Slavin as a useful way of advancing Dewey's investigative philosophy of primary schooling is little different from what is commonplace in English schools. 'Group Investigation' involves students identifying topics for study and then planning out a research programme. They then collaborate in the investigation, prepare and present a report, which is then evaluated by the teacher, by the group and by the other children in the class.

> For example, if the class were studying South America, different groups might choose different countries, or one group might choose the physical geography of South America, another the natural resources, and so on (Slavin, 1990, p.97).

This sounds like a disaster in the making. Not only does the method lack the individual rewards for progress made in group-work, which is a fundamental principle of Slavin's earlier work, but it also lacks the clarity of purpose and procedure which Galton and Williamson (1992) see as essential if children are to give themselves wholeheartedly to group-work.

This is not tantamount to saying that group-work is inappropriate in the humanities. Writers on geography education continue to commend small-group talk.  Molyneaux and Tolley (1987) suggested the following nine ideas, although no research evidence that they are effective has been presented:

- buzzing – free talk in response to a stimulus;
- brain-storm;
- comparison activities;
- making predictions;
- sequencing;
- matching;
- designing – for example how to reclaim derelict land;
- decision-making;
- empathising – discussing how various parties in a situation feel about it.

Several of these activities might equally be presented as individual seat-work tasks, which might be more manageable for the teacher, if *potentially* less rewarding for the learners.  Well-designed research into techniques for teaching children to do some humanities work in groups and for using groups to examine differences of view is greatly needed.

## Games and simulations

School geography has long been associated with information technology (IT).  One aspect of that association was simulations and games, both being outgrowths of the post-war nomothetic, modelling approach to geography.  This approach had been there long before IT, and I have not-too-fond memories of running whole-class board simulations of the building of the American railroad system.

The claimed advantages are motivational as well as more obviously geographical.  Children involved in the Railway Game came to see that human decision-making shapes space, and in the process some understood why certain decisions were made and what their costs and benefits were.

In a review of research into the effects of simulations in general, VanSickle (1986) found that there appeared to be a small, positive change in attitudes to the subject of study, and a more pronounced, but still small and positive effect on the learners' retention of knowledge.

That should not, at this point, be interpreted to mean that simulations are a complicated way of making little differences.  What VanSickle's study was not able to do was to investigate the clarity of understanding of students who had participated in games and simulations. This is an important drawback in his work, since the intention in geography is not to use simulations to reinforce factual knowledge, but rather to deploy them to enhance understanding. Yet again, a research input is desirable.

*Advance organisers*

By advance organisers we mean things such as previews and headings. This concept comes from research into reading, where the general opinion is that learning is easier when the learner has been primed on the key ideas and structure of the material to be learned. Martorella (1991) noted evidence that advance organisers are beneficial in social studies, facilitating learning and the retention of material. Stoltman (1991) saw benefits specifically for geography learning.

One form of advance organiser deserves special comment, particularly with the growth of curricula which prescribe so many learning goals. It is helpful for children to know the purpose of a particular topic (Brophy, 1990a), not least because, as Tann (1987) showed, they form their own conceptions of the purpose, conceptions which are often at variance with the teachers'. If children believe that the purpose of a geography topic is to produce neat maps and to remember a list of the natural resources of South America, then the teacher's intention that they should understand the way the land is used and how conflicts can arise about it would be vitiated. However, here teachers need to be especially honest in their action research (or self-appraisal) because so often we proclaim one thing – that we want to encourage discussion – and under the press of coping with classroom urgencies we do another – tell children to make less noise. Small wonder that researchers so often fail to find evidence that practice does deliver what theory promises.

*Reading strategies*

Reading is thinking. It is far more than code-breaking. In this section I shall assume that children have gained some skill with reading as code-breaking, which is a prerequisite of so much work in the humanities.

One strategy for improving children's reading in geography is preparatory discussion of what they are to read, which might be regarded as a form of advance organiser (Camperell and Knight, 1991). Curtis (1991), writing about social studies for children with learning difficulties, commended structured reading, by which he meant that children should be taught to use the titles, subtitles, maps, charts and pictures as well as the body of text. Furthermore, post-reading recall, summary and review sessions were also seen as helpful. Another technique requires children to take notes, which helps them to recall what they have read (Martorella, 1991). Wittrock (1986) reported that where fourth graders were taught to make verbal and spatial links between what they read and their existing knowledge and experience, their comprehension was considerably greater than that of two control groups, which recalls the foregoing discussion of concept development.

There is a case for saying that texts have gone too far to try to conform to readability formulae and in the process have lost the power to help children to develop 'advanced reading skills'. Consider the National Curriculum for English (DES, 1989b). At level 4, which should be the norm for 11 year olds, children should be able to search for and locate information, and use inference, deduction and their previous reading experience. At level 5, which will be attained by perhaps a quarter of 11 year olds, they should be distinguishing between fact and opinion, forming opinions and substantiating them with reference to what they have read. Such reading skills embody central themes of the humanities and can best be developed in the normal process of humanities work – always assuming that the learning materials offer scope for their development. In other words we are not talking of reading across the curriculum so much as reading *through* the curriculum. Texts which are dominated by the double-page spread and readability formulae; texts which are a collection of bits; texts which have ignored evidence that interest and engagement affect readability more than the objective difficulty of the prose; such texts can impede the reading development which can be done so well through – and which is a necessary part of – the humanities.

*Metacognition*

Thinking about thinking is attracting increasing attention. I am using metacognition to describe the process of being aware of what one knows, both in terms of declarative knowledge, or propositions, and in terms of procedural knowledge, or knowledge of how to do things. Research into children's reading (Camperell and Knight, 1991) has suggested that children can read better if they are encouraged to pick, consciously, from a range of strategies and Parker (1991) reviewed evidence that metacognition could help children with social studies and concluded that it could be powerful, as long as children used metacognitive strategies in the context of a 'deep' study: 'deep' was used in contrast to the 'another lesson, another topic' syndrome, as a way of signalling that it is best to cover a narrower range of content than is customary but to do so in greater depth and with more thoughtfulness. Brophy (1990a) saw metacognition as a vital ingredient of learning in a subject which valued critical thinking and decision-making so highly, while Flavell (1985), who invented the term, thought that metacognitive skills should be taught directly, could be taught, and that the effects were beneficial. However, there is no reason to doubt that Goodlad's 1984 observation is still valid, namely that 'Notably absent were [pupil] responses implying the recognition of having acquired some intellectual power or done something creative' (p.234).

The way in which the English National Curriculum is expressed invites the development of metacognition in order to develop children's geography learning. The attainment targets spell out concepts and procedures which children are to learn, recognise and apply. In the past teachers might have exposed children to these concepts or procedures without making explicit to them what they were mastering. Lacking awareness of their own knowledge, it would hardly be surprising if children failed to apply that 'tacit knowledge'. On the other hand, the use of slogans, for example, to summarise what children have learned and to help children know what they know, is a powerful use of metacognition. And, to repeat a point, the National Curriculum puts a premium on such knowledge, not least because children are to be assessed in terms of their knowledge of the procedural and propositional attainment targets.

The Schools Council History 13–16 Project used a similar approach, so that students became familiar with mottoes like 'people make history'. The project evaluator feared that sometimes these phrases were used without understanding, but nevertheless concluded that project students showed a superior grasp of history to non-project students (Shemilt, 1980). It is bold to claim that the use of metacognitive strategies accounted for the difference, but it is reasonable to make the more modest observation that in the project both teachers and students were encouraged to be both clear and explicit about what they were doing, to reflect on it, and to apply learned procedures and slogans.

Implicit in this discussion has been the idea that metacognition is subject-specific, that is to say that there are ways of working and concepts in geography which need to be learned, practised and consciously deployed. These, it has been implied, are different from the procedures and concepts applicable to English, or history, for example. This echoes the domain-specific view of children's learning which was reviewed in Chapter 4. Without denying the domain-specific element of understanding, and hence of metacognition, the other point of view should be heard, namely that

> some of these learning strategies and metacognitive processes will generalise across different subject matters. Knowledge about learning how to learn may be useful in a variety of school-related areas, may apply across several subjects taught in schools, and may be useful with different ability levels (Wittrock, 1986, p.310).

It will be argued in Chapter 9 that the same processes of enquiry and reflection are common to many primary school subjects, which implies that metacognition should have cross-curricular *and* domain-specific aspects. The former may provide a good way of integrating a primary curriculum, and we shall need to consider cross-curricular thinking programmes of the sort developed by Lipman, Feuerstein and DeBono.

## Gender differences

Mention has been made of some gender-related differences. The very way in which geography has been defined as a subject, with its emphasis on the geometry and mathematics of space, which might be characterised as 'masculine', may work against girls, who are held to incline towards people, lived experience and the human elements of values issues. These are matters which are not prominent in the English National Curriculum, and which have been overshadowed in academic geography by the quantifiers. Relph (1976) made a strong case for seeing place in highly human terms, claiming that

> Places ... are full with meanings, with real objects, and with ongoing activities. They are important centres of individual and communal identity, and are often profound centres of human existence to which people have deep emotional and psychological ties ... our relationships with places are just as necessary, varied, and sometimes perhaps just as

unpleasant as our relationships with people (p.141).

At an Oxford seminar on models in geography Cosgrove (1989) made a plea for the sense of place to be restored to geography, emphasising the effective and sensuous side of the study. It was a plea that was curtly despatched in the summary of the proceedings (Macmillan, 1989). Is geography, in its quest for academic respectability, becoming a 'masculine' subject? There do not appear to be research papers on this issue.

A final aspect of gender issues in geography concerns the way in which women have been represented in geography texts. Like history texts, geography books have reflected their times (Hicks, 1981; Marsden, 1988; Walford, 1989), jingoism, chauvinism, stereotypes, prejudice and all. Are geography books nowadays gender-fair? And of equal significance, are they culture-fair too, freed from the stereotypes of sinister Soviets, evil Arabs and idle Indians? Research has not yet been done on the English texts for the 1990s but if geography is first and foremost about people, it is essential to be clear about the sort of biases which are present in our public representation of other people to our young. And too often one of these representational biases is a gender bias, such that women's roles and lives are undervalued, underexamined and underanalysed.

## Summary

Just as the evidence used in this chapter has been international, so too the findings have an international consistency about them. Primary geography has been neglected, and when it has been noticed it has seldom been well done by.

We have seen that worthwhile geography is within the reach of primary school children, although, following Chapter 2, it needs to be sustained by a system-wide and school-wide commitment in which whole-school planning and whole-school learning are crucial. This may be threatened by the press of other priorities, particularly as schools feel compelled to concentrate on the 'basics'. However, this may be turned to good advantage since English, for instance, needs to be developed within the rich contexts provided by the social studies.

It is important that we are purposeful in our geography teaching, abandoning the old view that simple exposure to content is sufficient. It is not. As we saw in Chapter 4, meaningful learning and understanding depend on children forming connections and generating meanings, which implies far more purposive teaching strategies than have been common, hitherto. That is not to deny the theme of Chapter 3, that there are many ways of being effective in teaching, for this is as true of geography as of teaching in general. It is to qualify that general proposition by insisting that a concern for meaning-making must underpin whatever varied methods we use in primary geography.

The significance of human and values issues, both in the academic discipline and in the primary school subject, has been asserted. This, it has been shown, has implications for the teaching methods used.

If the promise of primary geography is to be fulfilled, action is needed on three fronts. First to make it a fair subject – to people of different cultures, to girls and boys, and to children with special educational needs. It is intolerable that a humanity subject should be anything other than humane. Secondly, the quality and quantity of classroom resources need to be improved. Thirdly, teachers' professional development needs to be enhanced, certainly through increasing their knowledge of the subject, but also through principled attempts to learn by and from systematic enquiries in classrooms – from action research.

Is history similarly placed?

# Chapter 7

# The Study of History

## The discipline

History has generally been seen as a distinct, autonomous discipline (e.g. Collingwood, 1946; Gardiner, 1952), resembling, yet set apart from, the social sciences, geography, fiction and biography. However, this consensus conceals differences of opinion. Where Oakeshott (1983) said that history was marked by its key ideas, such as 'change', 'happening', 'cause' and 'past', Mink (1973) dwelt upon its characteristic narrative form and Lee (1983) pointed to history's 'narrative structure, colligatory organisation, its concern with human action and rational explanation' (p.48). Moreover, some noted that history has many forms – legal, political, social, art, economic, demographic, for example – and argued that these shared only a family identity, that history is a polymorphous concept (Walsh, 1967; Tosh, 1984).

History, then, may be established as a subject and it may be distinguished by its concern with the past (and so it could be said to include geography), but as with geography, we notice a range of concerns such that the discipline immediately appears to be an integrating one. All and any human experience may be the concern of history, although the English government insists that English high school students study nothing which has happened in the past twenty years.

Time may be the dimension in which historians operate, but it does not define history. In one sense time is the historian's reference system, a way of identifying the order in which things appeared, and a way of identifying which phenomena might be associated with which others. The historian need not *understand* time, any more than a geographer needs to *understand* space. She needs to be able to *use* the temporal (or spatial) filing system. In the words of Fines (1982, p.115) 'I am not sure whether I can *understand* a century, even though I could make a stab at defining it'.

Nor is history about sources. Truly the historian depends on the leftovers from the past, on the surviving sources; agreed, many have not survived, and the remnants have often been changed by rats, flood, fire and decay; undoubtedly, those sources are bitty, seldom showing much of the lived experience of women, peasants, children and the old; and certainly they are replete with bias. Truly, the problems of source handling are so crucial to the discipline that historians have developed methods to try fairly to win the best from all sorts of sources, but it is a mistake to suppose that these rules of procedure define the study of history. Were that the case, history would be a methodology without a purpose, means whose sole end was better means.

Besides, it has been argued that, philosophically, there is nothing particularly awkward about *historical* sources. Atkinson (1978, p.41) argued that statements about the past 'are not generally to be contrasted unfavourably with similar statements about the present'. Bloch had taken a similar line, arguing that 'A good half of all we see is seen through the eyes of others ... In this respect the student of the present is scarcely better off than the historian of the past' (1954, pp.49, 50).

The past and the present may be seen as a continuum, which means that just as understandings of the present are acts of interpretation in varying degrees, so too are understandings of the past. In daily life interpretations might be more readily checked against experience. The past is another culture to us, and the more distant past is known through shreds, but as with the present, to try to understand it is to interpret the evidence. In practice there are facts of history, but the nub of the discipline is the disputed connections between those facts (did the expulsion of the French from North America produce the War of Independence?); the discussions of their meanings (was the American Constitution evidence of a belief in human rights?); and the evaluation of whether 'facts' can be accepted as 'facts' (was King Harold killed by an arrow at the Battle of Hastings in 1066?).[1]

'Laws' and 'lessons' are not the outcome. In history – and in human affairs generally – a 'cause' is 'no more than an expression of the concern of a historical enquiry to seek significant relationships between events' (Oakeshott, 1983, p.88). When we speak of causes, we speak of connections of shifting, subjective significance. And 'what they are is how they come to be woven' (*ibid*, p.63), with the historian as the

---

1 No – on two, maybe three grounds.

84

weaver.

So, history is a discipline with so many uncertainties that it has been described as 'a pack of tricks we play on the dead' (Voltaire, cit Marwick, 1970, p.78). Its purpose is not directly to teach us lessons, nor to form laws which show the future. Rather, the past is to be studied on its own terms and 'from within': the intention is to try to recreate the understandings, the perspectives of people in the different societies which constitute the past. History, then, is a multicultural study. Like geography, its goal is to try to explain (often strange) others on their own terms, within their own cultures, set in their situations, and without the benefit of hindsight.

Understanding and explanation in history rest on two simple premises: that people in the past may, in principle, be understood because they were human; and that their perspective differed from the historian's. Reconstructing that perspective involves making meaning out of whatever sources there are, which is itself an act of interpretation. The other act of interpretation follows as the historian tries to fathom the practical inference schema – the logic-in-use – which guided action.

Of course, history is not entirely concerned with accounting for action. It is also about producing description and about noticing changes and similarities over time. There is also a place for the emotional appeal of history, for vicarious joy, for sadness: room to be thrilled and to be engaged by a story. Some caution is needed when addressing the affective, or emotional, side of history. Sympathy can get mightily in the way of understanding and the historian is warned to guard against the biasing influence of such emotions. She may indeed sympathise with the underdog and the oppressed. It does not get her very far in explaining why they were oppressed, contributing little to reconstructing either the thinking of the oppressor or the behaviour of the oppressed. If empathy is defined as the attempt to understand people in the past, then it is an imperfect word to describe the core of history. If it is confused with sympathy, it is a rotten core (Knight, 1989b).

Five conclusions may be drawn out of this account of the discipline:

● history cannot ignore time, but time is not the object of the historian's attention;
● historians have problems with their sources, but important though their methods for handling them are, the methods do not define the discipline;
● the subject matter of history is anything human that has happened in the past, so it may be taken as an integrating subject;

● history is quintessentially about people;
● its concern with human thought and action and their effects places it alongside geography.

## The primary school study

### Its history

It is not surprising to find that the history of primary school history shows changing ideas about its place and its teaching. In 1894 *Philips' Picturesque History of England* said that

> a faithful record of what has been done by Englishmen for England is full of the best lessons for English boys and girls ... it is hoped that those who read this book will be enabled to understand with what wise beneficence God has ordered every part of the upbringing and education of our country, to fit it to perform its solemn duties to itself and to the whole world (Preface).

*Modern Teaching*, published in 1928, said that 'stories should be drawn from the *whole range of history*; the *romantic element* should predominate', with social and local history taught as '*illustrating the national story*'. 'History is an instrument of *moral training*'. Accordingly, 52 junior school topics were covered, the last of which dealt with 'A Great General: Earl Haig' (p.107). In this way history, like geography, was represented as a form of citizenship education.

The 1937 Board of Education *Handbook of Suggestions* repeated that 'In Literature, History and Geography the human and romantic features have at this stage the greatest appeal' (p.115). 'First hand experience is obviously impossible for the child [aged up to 15], who must depend upon his teacher or books for his knowledge of facts and events and of the relations between them' (p.401). While the content was to be nationalist, delivered largely through biography, 'it should be possible for children to see such parts of our history as are parts of world movements in due proportion' (p.417).

In the *Handbook of Suggestions*, as in *A Year in the Infant School* (which I date as a 1920s work) nothing was said about infant history: presumably too hard for infants, and too remote from the conception of 'the curriculum a matter not of subjects but of experience and activities' (p.85).

The accepted conceptions of primary history changed in post-war England, with a growing emphasis being laid on local history, on the use of sources, and on the metaphor of detective work (Blyth *et al*, 1976). Moreover, the interesting claim was made that 'it is possible to teach them [infants] how the historian functions' (Blyth, 1977, p.51). Practice trailed this thinking. In 1978 HMI reported that in 80 per cent of the primary classes which they had surveyed history was superficial, often amounting to little more than copying from text books, which themselves were unimpressive narratives. Later surveys endorsed this, as did my study of 100 inspection reports published in 1984/5 (Knight, 1988).

Yet a renaissance is apparent: most obviously in the English National Curriculum, but also in the Scottish proposals, in France (Marbeau, 1988), Canada (Clarke *et al*, 1990), New Zealand (McCulloch, 1992) and the USA (Bradley Commission, 1988).

## *Its nature*

Initially the English National Curriculum implied that children might spend 10 per cent of their time on history work, although ministers subsequently found it prudent to abandon such calculations.

In the infant years (DES, 1991c) children study history within living memory, hear stories about famous men and women, and do some work on a patch of the past beyond living memory (Knight, 1992).

In the junior years, for ages 7–11, children study five or six 'core' topics, which are predominantly Anglocentric, although the prescribed 'Explorations and Encounters c1450 – c1550' mysteriously brings Iberia to the fore, and a Hellenic topic is also prescribed. The remaining three or four units entail at least one study of developments over a millenium (from a list of six), at least one study on a non-European civilisation (from a list of six), and at least one unit based on a school-devised local study.

Children will be assessed against the five themes of the history attainment targets: they should develop a knowledge of chronology and an awareness of change; have some grasp of cause and consequence; acquire an awareness of differences; acquire an understanding that history deals in a variety of points of view and perspectives; and demonstrate an ability to use historical sources.

The distinctive feature of this curriculum is not the oddball content menu but the way in which it values the concepts and methods identified as central to history as an academic discipline.

Some of the criticisms of it resemble those made of the geography curriculum, but the issue of content knowledge also arose because the history curriculum was more prescriptive here than the geography curriculum. Strong views were expressed about what history children should learn, hence what view they ought to get of the sort of culture that England has. Some also wanted content knowledge to be assessed but others said that doing so would reduce history to lists of facts to be learned. Practical difficulties were seen, particularly in small primary schools where mixed age classes would be thrown into chaos by any requirement that a topic would be assessed only at a certain range of levels of attainment. The result might be that two or three history topics might have to be taught to different groups of children within the same mixed-age class. A lively, rather futile debate about the meaning of empathy in history ran through the quality press, some seeing any mention of empathy as a symptom of slack practice, low standards and child-centred vacuousness. The word did not appear in the National Curriculum.

The Scottish proposals (Scottish Office, 1992) also required children to acquire a grasp of chronology and of change, to learn about their heritage (which seems to be defined in narrow, Scottish terms), and to grapple with causation. Ideas about decision-making and points of view seem to be located more within the study of contemporary rather than past situations, and the idea of historical enquiry is embodied under a general heading of 'finding out', which returns us to the interesting question of whether historical investigation is different from investigations in the present. The content was not prescribed in detail. Topics should be chosen to illustrate features of three of the following periods – before 400AD; 500AD–1700; 1700–1900; and the twentieth century – and should be predominantly local and Scottish in character, but including at least two studies on 'the European/Wider dimension' (p.61). Nothing was said about how long a topic should be. The Secretary of State for Scotland expressed concern lest history and geography might not figure in a sufficiently distinctive manner in the later stages of primary schooling.

The Bradley Commission (1988), convened in concern at the submersion of history within American social studies, identified thirteen outcomes of school history, including an understanding of change, of causation, of the influence of individuals on history, of the elements of uncertainty and arationality in human affairs, and of diversity; children should also have empathy, rather than just present-mindedness, should understand people's common humanity, and recognise the interplay between history and geography.

While criticising the expanding horizons approach, arguing that children can reach out 'far beyond the limitations of the child's own family and community to the exciting worlds of history, biography and mythology' (1988, p.16), the Commission did not prescribe content, instead suggesting three, loose structures for work in the elementary years. However, it did insist that the social studies curriculum in the elementary years should be dominated by history and that national history should be complemented by work on other nations.

Some of its critics were concerned that the Commission's emphasis on story would lead to didactic history, while others (Evans, 1989) argued that 'more history, particularly "tell a story" history, is not the answer. History does not seem real to students ... the net result will likely be reinforcement of history as trivia' (p.88). Thornton (1990) also wondered whether giving history greater prominence in the curriculum would necessarily be an improvement, arguing that,

> re-arranging the number and structure of history courses appears to be less important than using scarce educational dollars to help teachers keep the curricular-instructional gate in as thoughtful fashion as they can (p.57).

In other quarters there was opposition to the premise that the social studies should be dismembered.

Five concluding points are:

- history has become an issue of concern in primary education, internationally. Something of a resurgence may be seen;
- primary history is about people, understanding, explanations and sources;
- as such, it sponsors sophisticated cognitive activities;
- there is national variation in what is taught;
- the notion of 'good practice' in history, as in general (Alexander, 1992), is a slippery one, a matter of what fits the educational understanding of the dominant forces here and now.

*Chapter 8*

# History in the Primary School

## What has been taught and how

In general the picture for history is much as that for geography. Five points are developed below.

### Neglect

There is almost as great a dearth of research into primary history as into primary geography. There were 230 entries in the 1992 ERIC catalogue and, coincidentally, 230 in BEI for 1986–91. The proportion of these entries which seemed to be research-based was also similar to that for geography.

Just as we have seen that geography was little taught in primary schools in England in the 1980s, so too with history (DES, 1989a; HMI, 1990). In the USA Levstik and Yessin (1990) noted that it was often relegated to short parts of the afternoons.

### Localism

Because history was seen as a vehicle for general skills development and because it was one of the 'afternoon' subjects it was unusual for people to discuss what history content children ought to study. If the question was asked, the answer tended to be that local and recent history was appropriate.

In 1987 I surveyed 81 primary teachers keen enough on history to attend a history conference. I found that 44 per cent of the topics which they had taught in the previous year were on local and recent themes, while 25 per cent were loosely attached to titles such as 'change' or 'water'. A 1988/9 study of 28 teachers in northwest England who were identified as skilled in history work found that 43 per cent of observed topics were definitely about local and recent issues, while 51 per cent of the topics which were mentioned in interviews fell into that category. This bears out the conclusion drawn in a study of 100 school inspection reports published in 1984/5 that topics often appeared to be suggested by TV series or to be based on the locality and the recent past (Knight, 1988). Elsewhere, 'critics have long accused US social-studies instruction of being shamefully chauvinistic and ethnocentric' (Mehlinger, 1991, p.455).

This narrowing of history, inherent in the misnamed 'expanding horizons' model illustrates the way an academic subject may be transformed on its journey into the classroom.

*Wider horizons*

Development education and world studies were both popular in some English primary schools, both should have had a strong history dimension, but didn't. As a result there were two ways in which foreign history crept in. One was the inevitable historical dimension to topics on 'China', 'Spain', 'Mexico' or whatever other country caught the teacher's fancy. This usually amounted to a compilation of not-very-fascinating facts from poor-quality books, leading to compilations of trivia, nicely illustrated. The themes of 'me and my family' or 'people on the move' were another way in which non-British history might be raised, especially in schools situated in ethnically diverse areas.

*Teaching and learning methods*

There is evidence that teachers dominated history classes in England as they did geography, with the recitation lesson alive and well (Knight, 1991a). American evidence described indifferent practices, often influenced by indifferent textbooks (Brophy, 1992). It is important, though, to repeat that the recitation, direct instruction approach is not necessarily doomed to lead to dull work, although it is not best suited to all the sorts of learning one seeks in school history. In particular, the concern with the surface feature of content acquisition can deflect the teacher from developing general understandings and metacognitive awarenesses.

Yet, many interesting techniques have been reported which mark a vibrant break from exposition, text processing and drawing, even if they have not been widely used. So, there are accounts of work with computers – on census data, to model castle-building and to create 'newsroom' simulations; of on-site work where children look for evidence of change and past usage, see how a castle might be attacked – or defended – re-enact daily life, plan a tourist trail, try to reconstruct the place as once it was; of class museums and artefact-based enquiries; of oral history projects, piecing together the past and finding that two grannies will disagree, as sources in general are wont to; of structured dilemmas, where children try to work out historical problems; of older children reading and writing history for younger ones; of the use of fiction; of drama being treated as a stimulus to research and as a means for collaborative problem-working; of the use of sets of documentary and/or pictorial sources; of timelines; and so on (Knight, 1991; Cooper, 1992).

I want to make four points about such methods. First, they are not endemic. Secondly, they are most easily applied to local and recent topics. Thirdly, many published classroom materials rely on busy-work activities rather than such demanding and engaging activities. And lastly, whatever techniques are used, teachers need to seize hold of the central ideas (about Stuart times, say, and about points of view(AT2) and about effective reading strategies) and structure the work so that these, rather than the trivia, are what children take away with them.

## Assessment

These teachers had almost invariably cited children's interest, engagement and enthusiasm as criteria by which the success of history work should be judged. Distinctive history criteria were not mentioned. It is not surprising, then, that in the teaching study, assessment, where it was apparent, was rarely based upon history criteria: detailed history criteria ... were even less in evidence ... Teachers were [also] asked whether children had made progress during the lesson and how they knew that to be so ... [Their] responses were mainly (and confidently) undifferentiated ... 30% of answers said that their assessment of progress had been based on children's level of engagement; 35% had been influenced by children's oral questions, answers and discussions; 20% had looked at children's written work ... Strikingly absent is evidence of children's *progress* in learning and evidence of what children *had learnt* (Knight, 1991a, p.134).

Brophy (1990a) noted that in American social studies assessment it was objective, comprehension questions which predominated, the 'higher order' elements being neglected. His preference was to ask 'students to work on tasks calling for holistic demonstration of meaningful understanding of content and ability to apply it using important skills and strategies' (p.408).

## Why was history taught like this?

All that was said about why geography was taught as it commonly has been can be applied to history.

## Harbingers of better practice

The same can be said here too.

## A research context

### Time

Whitrow (1988) has shown that time is a culturally constructed concept, that 'there is no unique intuition of time that is common to all mankind' (p.10). This is a useful reminder that discussion of children's understanding of time cannot reasonably be separated from consideration of what they have been taught. Since little history has been taught to elementary school children, it is quite possible that reports that they have little grasp of historical time reflect the curriculum, not their capacity.

That should be kept in mind when considering a research review (Thornton and Vukelich, 1988) which reported that at the age of seven (surely much earlier?) children can correctly sequence members of their family; at age eight, they can correctly order dates (surely a mathematical, not a time ability?); at age nine can use general time terms, such as long ago (again, surely misplaced?), and also can say how many years ago something was; and at age ten can label periods of time such as the Civil War years.

Surprisingly this review did not include West's important work (1981), in which he examined whether children could become better at sequencing historical materials, at forming sets of materials from the same time, and at identifying authentic materials. He was not obsessed by the number of time but concentrated on the structure of temporal understanding. He certainly showed that narrow application of partly understood Piagetian notions 'consistently ... under-rate the skills and understanding of the concrete operational stage ... denigrated their [children's] ability in logical thinking' (p.368), but the results of formal testing showed only a 10 per cent improvement in the group exposed to his special curriculum, which was 'hard-earned and not always dependable ... they were, on occasions, overtaken by the control group' (p.357). Nevertheless, he certainly demonstrated that junior school children can achieve an understanding of chronology sufficient for them to undertake demanding and worthwhile history work, a finding which has significantly influenced the English National Curriculum.

*Understanding people in the past*

In Chapter 7 it was claimed that history involves understanding people in the past, although that phrase has been criticised for looseness by Cooper (1992), who prefers the term 'empathy'. Whatever term is used, there is a measure of agreement about what primary school children can achieve in this area of understanding.

Cooper (1992, p.343) has insisted that the 'development of historical empathy is not a separate process from interpreting evidence', which is consistent with the argument set out in Chapter 7. Knight (1988) argued that children in Key Stage 2 could recognise that characters in the past had perspectives different from theirs; could venture explanations which depended on taking another's perspective; could likewise attempt to predict the outcome of a situation; and could make evaluations of historical characters which involved handling evidence which could support more than one judgement. A developmental sequence was identified, and it was argued that children could be accelerated through that sequence by crafty teaching. Person-centred history work would seem to be possible, even rewarding, with children of this age. In fact infants also coped with a people-centred course on the Middle Ages, a topic which might have been misunderstood to lie outside the realms of concrete operational thinking. He also found smaller than expected differences between children's understanding of people in the past and their understanding of people in the present who they had not met, which echoes some of the geography research reviewed in Chapter 6.

Like Cooper, he was unsure of the value of story writing as a means of exercising what she called 'empathy', arguing that structured dilemmas, role-taking exercises, drama, reason-seeking, shifting patterns of group work, and teaching for 'thoughtfulness' were effective ways of enhancing children's understanding of people in the past – and in the present, too.

## Concept development

In a rather oddly formed study Coltham (1960) examined children's (whose mean age was 10 years and eleven months) understanding of six concepts (king, invasion, ruler, subject, early man, trade) and concluded that 'the general level of attainment apparently typical of the age-group is less advanced in the field of history than in fields of knowledge where first-hand experience is possible' (p.219). However, other studies have suggested that children might cope better with history concepts than early research suggested. We have noted West's work on time concepts, and should notice Booth's work with adolescents (1979) which indicated that they could form concepts to relate different pieces of historical evidence.

More recently Cooper, working with Y4 children, deliberately taught them a series of concepts associated with each of four study units. The unit on the stone age contained 22 concrete concepts (of which *hachure* is a notable example), 14 abstract concepts (including 'tools', 'shelter' and 'weapons') and 21 superordinate concepts (for example 'palaeolithic', 'ritual', 'domesticate'). Children had to use the concepts, particularly in discussion, and were encouraged to forge connections between them. Most of the taught concepts were, she reported, spontaneously used by children, who learned to do this regularly. This, she said, helped their historical reasoning by extending the possibilities available to them.

There appears to be some tension between her findings and the criticism that introducing too many concepts in a shallow 'cultural literacy' programme is ineffective and pointless (Downey and Levstik, 1991). However, although Cooper bombarded the children with concepts, care was taken that they were explained, applied to concrete materials, preferably reinforced through fieldwork and used in group discussions where children were encouraged to make connections and to search for likenesses below the surface. It is the purposeful and thoughtful attention to concept development which distinguishes Cooper's work and which is consistent with the view of concept development which has already been outlined.

## Reasoning in history

Historical reasoning, with its emphasis on making connections and weaving meanings, certainly has a strong element of imagination about it. That has led some, such as Booth (1979), to reject attempts to locate historical understanding within a general developmental framework, of which Piaget's is an example. Indeed, the results of early 'Piagetian' research into historical understanding were discouraging, showing that formal operational reasoning in history became evident long after it was apparent in mathematics, that concrete operational thinking in history was also delayed, and that little could be done to close the gap through good teaching (Hallam, 1975). I suspect that these sets of results may be the product of misinterpretations of Piaget's ideas, and elsewhere (Smith and Knight, 1992) evidence is presented that for adolescents the gap between 'Piagetian' and history tasks is slight.

It is equally important to insist that researchers such as Blyth (1977), Booth (1979), West (1981) and Cooper (1992) have shown that children in the elementary school can achieve worthwhile historical understandings. Cooper has also shown that their reasoning can be simply supported by worksheets which encourage them to examine sources with three questions in mind (what do you know for certain about it? what can you guess? what would you like to know?), each of the three questions being associated with the invitation to draw a conclusion or to give a reason for their statement. Similar prompts were also extensively used by West (1981) and Knight (1988), who also found that teaching improved children's ability to internalise and use the prompts.

## Distant times

The phrase 'concrete operational stage' is most unfortunate, encouraging the belief that children in primary schools need to encounter things in the flesh, as it were, to understand them.

Egan (1979) proclaimed his belief in the vigour of children's mental worlds with their dichotomies between good and evil, weak and strong, heroic and cowardly, arguing that teaching should use the story format to build on that fascination. Brophy (1990a) also noted the claim 'that primary school children are interested in stories about heroes, the exotic and the long ago and far away' (p.357). Since children come to school already having a heap of knowledge about the past, from TV if from nowhere else, and since in language work it is accepted that children have rich powers of imagination, it does seem reasonable to think that the expanding horizons view may not tell the full story of the development of historical understanding, which could equally well be represented as an interplay between the nearly here-and-now and the far distant.

Evidence has already been seen that Key Stage 1 children can make some sense of the Middle Ages and Levstik and Yessin (1990) described a Y1 topic on Columbus, which was presented as an example of good practice. With regard to geography and history, more needs to become known about learning and teaching content which is not based upon the child's immediate, sensuous surroundings.

*Questioning; games, simulations and IT; advance organisers; reading strategies; metacognition*

The degree of overlap in research into humanities subjects is considerable, and most of what was said about these topics under the heading of geography can be repeated for history too, but a couple of things about reading and metacognition need to be added.

For example, Fines (1992) has insisted that history should not be too easy, and taken issue with school texts which are often simplified at the expense of colour and challenge. 'Teaching children to read intelligently has become a focal point of the Primary History Project' (p.39). In less robust terms the Bradley Commission (1988) also called for reading to be emphasised in history learning, while Downey and Levstik (1991) said that reading and discussing historical fiction and biography could encourage children to interpret and analyse textbook versions of the past. Levstik and Yessin (1990) argued that history can be used to promote whole language and thought development in Key Stage 1 and that it is, in turn, advanced by methods which encourage children to read purposefully and thoughtfully. Brophy (1990b) described the same approach in fifth grade.

However, research into American elementary school history texts has pointed to deficiencies which limit the potential for reading and history to be mutually re-inforcing (White, 1988). While Brophy and colleagues (1991) recognised the face validity of calls for more detailed and personalised reading materials, they concluded that history texts should make more realistic assumptions about children's prior knowledge, identify key ideas and structure the material around them, and make connections among concepts, using advance organisers in the process. Sources should be more prominent and a range of perspectives should be seen. In short, more emphasis needed to be placed on producing texts which encouraged children to structure knowledge, learn metacognitive strategies, think critically and apply their conclusions in decision-making. Thornton (1990) was more sceptical, arguing that change should concentrate on teachers, not texts. English materials supporting the National Curriculum differ in important ways from American materials but I rather suspect that they are faulty in their own ways.

It seems to be becoming more usual to make it clear to children what they are doing and learning, and why. The Bradley Commission had said that children should understand why history is studied, which is a first step on the way to helping children to see connections within the study and to learning appropriate procedures and concepts to apply. Fines (1992) reported that in his Primary History Project children were being told about the goals of the ATs in a modified form, so that they knew what the teachers were looking for. Cooper (1992) was sure that children 'need to be explicitly aware of what they are learning to do, why it is important, and what the next step may be' (p.167). Wineberg worked from the proposition that there is a domain-specific form of enquiry and argued that students needed to learn how to read texts in a historical mode and that,

> high school is too late to begin teaching children to ask one set of questions of a short story and another set of their history book; they must learn to ask such questions when they first encounter claims about the past (1991, p.25).

He did not naively claim that metacognitive awareness would of itself solve the problem of history learning but he certainly believed that it should be deliberately developed.

Slavin (1990) has given examples of the use of group-work methods in history learning. Unfortunately, they are not examples of his preferred methods, STAD and TGT (see Chapter 6), but of the far weaker method which he called Jigsaw II. One primary school unit was on the Blackfoot Amerindian and the second was a high school unit on the Cold War. Mixed ability groups of children were assigned different sections of text on the topic which they had to master. In the class as a whole there would be several children, working in a group on the same section of text. They were grouped together to discuss what they had read and to help each other to understand it. In this way every child was a member of an 'expert group' before returning to their team and presenting to the team a report on the material which they had mastered, so that everyone in the team was a tutor on one 'minitopic' and a learner about all the others. All children were then tested on the whole of the topic and when the tests had been marked, scores were assigned to each child in proportion to the *progress* which each had made on the topic. A child whose work had improved might have gained a higher score for his team than one whose marks were higher but whose work was no better on this occasion than it was on the last occasion. Team scores were then computed and compared.

The problem with this use of Jigsaw II is that it is framed around the goal of understanding a narrative text. If history – or geography – is seen as a different sort of study, then the Jigsaw II method seems to be less appropriate. Moreover, the test presented by Slavin (p.165) is a multiple-choice, objective answer test, which is generally (but not invariably) not the best way to assess historical understanding. So, we see again the paradox that group-work is thought to be particularly appropriate to subjects where judgement, hypothesising, evaluation and interpretation are all prized, yet the most sophisticated research has it taking place within the context of more 'closed' subject matter.

Cooper (1992) has also argued that children working in unsupervised groups produced, spontaneously, more suggestions than did teacher-led groups, although they were less systematic in pursuing those ideas. Unled discussions were valuable in enabling children to correct each other, to express ideas in their own way and to clarify and control their own thinking. She saw both led and unled discussion as important ways of enhancing eight and nine year olds' historical thinking.

Short-lived, shifting groupings can be a powerful way of engaging children, of encouraging the cognitive conflict which was identified as being so important in Chapter 2, and of supporting those important 'higher order skills'. Fines (1992) has reported that productivity in history classrooms has improved when groups of 4–10 have been divided up into pairs – or into singletons.

An example of such temporary, shifting grouping would be where children were asked to decide which of, say, five things was the main outcome of the development of the railway in the nineteenth century. They could then briefly be grouped together according to their preferred choice, and told to work out a case to explain why their chosen consequence was the best choice. The teacher might prompt, feed in supplementary material and encourage children to look at the faults with the other four possibilities. Then these temporary groups would be dissolved and children put in threes, say, with each child representing a different preference. At the end of about ten minutes each three would vote to show which of the five consequences it thought the most important.

Another form of temporary grouping is known as pyramidding. Children work in pairs or threes, and the groups are then merged into fours or sixes, with instructions to agree or to select the most important points from the ideas generated by the two smaller groups. This can be carried on with the fours joining to form eights and so on, but I find that the law of diminishing returns – and diminishing interest – soon applies.

General principles may be abstracted from the research: rules of working in groups need to be learned, for (male) children do not necessarily take to collaboration; work needs to be assigned to individuals but groups will be judged on the product of the work of all the individuals in the group; it can be useful to combine home-base and expert groupings; groups may compete with each other. Unfortunately, we still lack well-formed humanities investigations of the impact of group-work which offer what research into STAD and TGT have provided for other subjects.

## Gender differences

At this age there is no consistent evidence that gender is related to performance in history, which may say more about the lack of research than anything else.

Differences in interest need to be investigated. J. Blyth (1977) reported differences in the interests of six-year-old girls and boys, but her sample was very small. Although teaching methods are likely to prove to be a confounding variable, with a sample of English primary teachers claiming that most history topics are potentially interesting (Knight, 1991a), the development of national curricula in the UK and the general revival of history mean that it is now both feasible and timely to consider whether history, as now conceived in several states, is more to the taste of girls or boys. It would also be worth seeking views about teaching techniques to see whether there are any gender differences in preferences.

The other points made under this heading in Chapter 6 apply here too.

## Summary

No longer just stories about great, dead, white Englishmen, history in the primary years is still about time (which really should not cause serious problems if treated in West's way) and people (who junior children can understand in some measure). Story has a place – an enlarged place, but children are now expected not just to receive the story but to reason about it (and there is evidence that they can reason serviceably with history materials). As for the content, in the UK that was decided by the government and in England there is force in the charge that dead white males still dominate the prescribed view of the past. Yet the National Curriculum has its virtues, rescuing primary history from neglect and parochialism, while imposing a structure which should make teaching more purposeful (at the expense of the 'exposure' view) and assessment more useful.

A theme of this chapter has been that we need to know a lot more about how children learn history and how it may be taught to good effect. Past, putative 'good practice' is no guide to the era of an objectives-led National Curriculum which demands that distant times and remote peoples be studied. As ever, a major element in this research will be the teaching professionals who systematically study their own practices, shaping those practices in the light of principles such as those described in Chapters 3 and 4.

But perhaps the most pressing need of all is work which helps others to see and use vivid, vibrant, vigorous and vital ways of teaching about distant times and distant places: a danger is that didactic, pencil-and-paper methods will take over, especially in history, where teachers' choice of content is more constrained than in geography. A second danger is that plenty of activities will be found on, say, the Ancient Egyptians, but that few will have historical value, being the educational equivalent of watching paint dry. There is some evidence that both dangers are pressing on primary history and primary geography.

And there is a third danger. Harried to deliver high standards in the 'basics', schools may sacrifice the foundation subjects to find the time for spelling bees, long division practice and learning science facts (the sun is a star). Where is the time to come from in which the humanities are to be enjoyed?

## Chapter 9

# *Arguments about Integration*

### Introduction

Both geography and history have their own distinctive features but there is also much common ground: both are human subjects; they share many ways of working; their content overlaps; and both are inherently integrating studies. Moreover, there has been a tradition in the primary years of adopting integrated approaches to the curriculum, teaching history and geography together through the social studies (as in the USA, Canada, Australia, New Zealand), or through environmental studies (Scotland), topics or project work (England).

In this chapter the powerful case against integration is reviewed, and it is argued that the problems are more ones of implementation than of conception – but that the problems are no less severe for that. The case for integration is then illustrated through accounts of different approaches to integration. Yet integration within the National Curriculum, although possible, is far from simple, and four powerful obstacles are noted – lack of resources, lack of rewards, lack of guidance and the pressure of other demands on teachers: the case for integration collapses unless these obstacles can be surmounted.

Chapter 10 gives examples of different ways of pursuing subject integration.

I shall tend to use the terms topic work, integration, social studies and project work interchangeably.

### A case against integration

something of an overblown fiction disguising undifferentiated business and slack assessment and diagnostic practice (P. Jackson, *cit* Burroughs, 1988, p.148).

Integration by content has often been shallow and contrived. Even if attention is shifted away from the content elements to the general skills which topic work is said to develop there is cause for concern. Having remarked that 'topic work often degenerated, both in my own classroom and in classrooms I observed ... into a rather uncritical quest for information and a heavy reliance upon limited resources', Long (1987, p.169) claimed that topic work did not necessarily support higher-order reading skills, nor research skills, nor was there evidence of any skills learnt being transferred to other contexts. Lewis (1987) looked at writing activities in Year 8 in humanities and in English and found that the humanities activities were characterised by copying, simple writing and comprehension. Drafting and redrafting were not used.

In some part this mismatch between the rhetoric of topic work and the practice may be because where teachers saw topics as ways for children to 'learn how to learn', children saw the purpose as to accumulate factual knowledge (Tann, 1987).

We have already seen evidence of concern in other countries that established social studies curricula are characterised by shallowness.

It is as if the quest for similarities as a basis for integration results in a drab mash in which the distinctive colours of the subjects have been lost and only the neutral tones of the common ground can be seen. The distinctive subjects lose their identity in the quest for the lowest common denominator around which integration can take place, as we saw in Chapter 6.

Writing of New Zealand, Low-Beer (1986) argued that a significant problem was that the social studies involved trying to match two fundamentally incompatible subjects, history and social science. The former lost. Likewise, writing of history in New Zealand primary schools Simon said,

> the social studies curriculum de-emphasises history 'knowledge' in favour of an emphasis on general understandings about human behaviour and values such as those relating to social justice, together with skills of critical enquiry (1992, p.268).

She used figures released by the Education Department in 1987 to show the predominance of the present in New Zealand primary social studies and the virtual absence of a temporal perspective – in F2 (children aged 10–11) 8 per cent of the social studies concerned New Zealanders in the past.

This lowest common denominator thesis has been endorsed by HMI, who echo Mortimore and colleagues (1988) in saying that topic work is difficult to manage (HMI, 1990), and add that it frequently lacks coherence and is fragmented. Elsewhere (DES, 1989a, p.8) they remark that 'satisfactory or good practice was often related to aspects of topic work *other than* history and geography'. This is consistent with the views of a team which recently reviewed the principal research evidence on English primary education (Alexander *et al*, 1992), who said that topic work was often not the product of integration but of non-differentiation, that is to say that it was the result of teachers' failure to recognise the distinctive subject perspectives and to plan for their development within the topic, to the benefit of the topic and of the subjects. They found unacceptable this *laissez-faire* approach to the way children construct meaning, and criticised the lack of planning which went with it.

We should also recall American evidence that the social studies, replete with ambitious aims, are frequently reduced to the lowest common denominator of the recitation approach (Chapters 6 and 8, above). To this might be added Bell's observations (1991) on European studies. Considerable importance has been attached to 'critical thinking', yet his reports of primary school work on Europe seem to show the priority given to the acquisition of knowledge, accompanied by practice in reference and recording skills.

One part of the problem may be that social studies courses are a relatively recent development, largely a product of the inter-war years, while England's affair with project and topic work is often traced to the Plowden Report of 1967. Lacking the gravity, traditions, status, standards and social networks of (somewhat) older subjects such as geography and history, it is claimed that integrated approaches are bound to be found wanting.

Yet, both history and geography are also relatively recent cultural constructs (Goodson, 1988) and have changed their shape during the twentieth century – and are plainly continuing to do so, both as academic subjects and as school studies. So, subject integration may lack quite the tradition of geography and history, but while that may help to explain the lack of resistance to disintegration, it does not seem able to account for its collapse.

One explanation of the threat to integration, internationally, may be that it is a fundamentally flawed concept.

The influential views of Hirst (1965) saw curriculum divided very much on subject-specific lines. This aligns with the position that school subjects should correspond, in some measure, to the mature academic subjects. An advantage of this correspondence theory is that the standards of school subjects may be calibrated against those embodied in higher education, so history and geography can be depicted as respectable and rigorous in ways which cannot be applied to 'topic' or 'project' work, or even to social studies (Mehlinger, 1991).

Some implications of this may be seen in Brophy's (1990a) claim that so far from being kindred, history and geography, as school subjects, are distinctly different from each other. Where history works by 'concretising' and personalising, by examining causes and trends, other social studies subjects incline to generalisation and key concepts, he said. It has been argued in Chapters 5 and 7 that this is by no means the only way in which these subjects can be seen, but here the point is that if one's epistemology is a separate subject epistemology, then there is a pronounced tension with integrated approaches: what philosophy has divided, let no-one join together?

The epistemological case for topic work always depended on advancing the claim that traditional, subject-centred forms of knowledge were arbitrary and that integrated forms (of which there were rather too many versions) were a better way of describing human knowledge. This was not the easiest position to propose and defend, and the complementary case, based on psychology, proved more persuasive.

From a psychological perspective, learning, it was said, is and should be child centred, and hence seamless. However, we saw that general theories of learning, such as those of Vygotsky and Piaget, have been challenged by domain-specific analyses. In other words, it is one thing to learn mathematics, and another to learn history. The two subjects have different concerns, different procedures, different typical misconceptions and different truth values. Native wit alone will not allow one to succeed in either subject, since mastery of the principles of the discipline, practice and rich subject knowledge are all necessary. This model of expertise as being steeped in a domain may be taken to imply that children will learn most effectively if they are required to work within a well-structured domain. Since it could be said that integrated approaches do not have this structure, it would follow that separate subject studies could prove psychologically more appropriate.

Teachers need to understand what is being integrated, and Bernstein (1975) argued that it is far more important for those working with integrated approaches to understand the 'deep structure' of each subject than it is for those teaching separate subjects. In Chapter 3 we looked at the complexity of subject matter knowledge and saw that often teachers are weak in this area. This is not a necessary state of affairs, but it does appear to be a common one, and it is easy to see that if a low-status area, such as social studies, demands that teachers become familiar with three disciplines (civics, geography and history) in order to teach it well then, realistically, those demands are going to be ignored. Moreover, it will be shown in Chapter 11 that in the UK neither initial teacher education, nor in-service provision have supported primary phase humanities. A major problem with integration is simply that it demands sharp subject matter understanding.

In 1946 Professor K. Cumberland, who held the chair of geography at the University of Auckland explained that an integration of history and geography was impossible since both were already extensive subjects. He said,

> when we realise that each field is theoretically as wide in phenomenal content as the sum of the systematic sciences, it becomes clear that in New Zealand the Thomas Report makes an almost impossible demand on our secondary school teachers and their pupils in requiring them to make a fusion of these and other subjects under the heading 'social studies' ... they may not be completely merged without losing what value they possess as cultural subjects, each making its distinctive contribution to the educational system (*cit* McCulloch, 1992, pp.176–7).

Interestingly, the very definitional problems which have caused so much uncertainty as to the meaning of geography and history, and which can be seen to provide a case for joining two interpenetrating studies, was here being used to explain why two synthesising subjects could not be joined.

Of course, some teachers are well informed, able to cut through complexity and can be an important source of advice for colleagues. However, the structure of the school is important here, since unless there is a system through which a semi-specialist teacher, or curriculum co-ordinator, can share expertise with colleagues, it is hard to see how progress will be made. Bernstein, in his seminal work (1975), emphasised the degree to which integrated approaches to the curriculum demand more tightly organised, cohesive and collaborative organisations, which returns us to the discussion of effective schools. Successful integration is a whole-school, not a one-teacher, affair.

Nevertheless, inspired materials, which in this context would promote topic approaches, can carry schools and teachers a long way.

Unfortunately, integrations tend to be eclectic, the fruit of school-based curriculum development. Often such topic approaches are supported only by teacher-produced materials and a collection of information books (often of dubious quality). Resources for locally based social studies are a particular problem, and published resources for any attempts to associate the social studies with others – such as the language arts – are strikingly absent. Even in the infant years, where such attempts are likely to come more naturally, there is a lack of resources, with David and colleagues (1992, p.13) deploring the lack of 'progressive, integrated packages that support simultaneous attention being given to subject materials, literacy and numeracy'.

Even where official policies sponsor cross-curricular approaches, through the social studies in the USA, for example, there is evidence that it is the more routine, easily managed, 'lower level' processes which are emphasised in the materials and in the pedagogy. In a sense, the social studies are collapsing in the face of market forces which subvert their very reason for being.

Subject integration, difficult to do in the balmy old days of teacher autonomy, has to compete with the other, formidable demands of the National Curriculum for the teacher's time. Where the government has produced advice on 'cross-curricular themes', it has been complicated, unsynchronised and unintegrated. In short, it encouraged teachers to check through what they had already planned to see where they had touched upon economic awareness or environmental education, but advance planning for a coherent cross-curricular theme was unattractive. Not only did it mean more work; not only did it mean re-thinking plans that had already been laid (because advice on cross-curricular themes lagged behind key subject curriculum requirements); and not only did it require jesuitical subtlety; but it is also hard to believe that many saw this 'patch and mend' approach to integration as desirable.

As we have seen, good quality integration (rather than the spatchcock which often passes for topic work) is inherently demanding and, by its very nature as a form of school-based innovation, unsupported by agencies outside the school. D. Hargreaves (1991, p.40) expected that 'a few schools or scholars will somehow salvage a holistic and coherent curriculum from the mountain of advice', but given the intensification of teachers' work over the past five years – and not only in the UK – he was right to wonder 'but will teachers then be in a mood to receive it?'.

In Chapter 3 we saw that a consequence of teachers feeling powerless to affect their working lives was a decline in their attempts to do so. A consequence of the deprofessionalising bureaucratisation of education –

and not just in England – could be a dwindling of those initiatives, of which subject integration is one, which have vivified schools and scholars, teachers and taught.

## Why integrate?

> The Plowden Report (1967) saw topic forms of work as vehicles for promoting flexibility in the primary curriculum ... and ... a means through which child-centred approaches could be realised. The learning of young children is not naturally differentiated, their view of the world is not divided into neat compartments ... children need the opportunity to range widely and freely over broad areas of experience if learning is not to become fragmentary and unrelated to their lived world. A topic approach ... stresses the process as well as the product of learning ... when based on direct experience the study can be geared to a child's developmental needs and interest ... By incorporating exploratory approaches the child becomes an agent in his [sic] own learning (Burroughs, 1988, p.151).

It is worth repeating that integration is taken to cover a range of practices, from tightly structured curricula like those embodied in American social studies texts, to the open-ended approach of individual project work, where topic, structure and integration come, if at all, from the child. Later, it will be important to comment on the ramifications of these different forms. First, seven grounds for integration are reviewed.

### Concepts

A concept-based approach to the curriculum implies an integrated approach.

The *Place, Time and Society 8–13 Project* (Blyth *et al*, 1976), like Bruner's *Man, a Course of Study,* was a project based on the belief that helping children to form concepts would prove to be more powerful than filling them with unorganised information. The Project list of seven sets of concepts may be divided into two sets: one being a set of broad substantive concepts, which included 'power' 'communication', 'consensus/conflict' and 'values/beliefs', with the other comprising key recurrent concerns of the social sciences, including 'causation', 'similarity/difference' and 'continuity/change'. These concepts crossed disciplinary boundaries, so that change, for example, is a historical concept but is obviously crucial in many other studies too.

*Problems*

In reality problems do not present themselves as geography, or engineering or sociology problems. 'A curriculum that aspires to promote problem-solving and encourages civic participation will find appropriate content from the natural sciences, from the humanities, and from popular culture' (Mehlinger, 1991, p.456). Not only are problems typically multi-disciplinary, but also one of the most important things for people to learn is how to work problems into forms where existing (disciplinary) tools will give some purchase on them.

Closely related to this idea is the theme of applying knowledge. Harling (1990) argued that the mathematics should be applied to practical, investigative, problem-working activities in a variety of contexts, which is strongly implied by maths AT 1. Much the same could be said of English.

If, the argument goes, knowledge is to be applied, especially to problem-working, then the situations to which it is applied will normally be 'cross curricular', for problems in life tend not to appear with subject labels neatly attached to them.

*Epistemological*

Just as there is a subject-based epistemology (Hirst, 1965), so too there are others which analyse knowledge into 'realms of meaning', for example (Phenix, 1964). The attractiveness of alternative epistemologies may be seen in the flirtation HMI had with Phenix' analysis until ministers broke off the engagement. Where a recent analysis of school geography (Morris, 1992) has argued that cross-curricular themes offer a powerful means of delivering a relevant, broad, balanced, coherent curriculum embodying continuity and progression, the alternative view that 'subjects are some of the most powerful tools for making sense of the world which human beings have ever devised' (Alexander *et al*, 1992, p.21), presently holds greater sway in official circles. That does not, of course, imply that alternative epistemologies are invalid: it quite simply casts them as *alternative* epistemologies – for the present.

*Psychological*

The quotation which heads this section makes several psychological claims for integration, referring particularly to theories of the ways children construct meaning, and of motivation. It is true that young children do not see the world in differentiated subject terms, although one job of education is to lead them from indifferentiation to differentiation: the question then becomes one of the age at which particular forms of differentiation are best introduced. In the primary years there is no good reason to think that differentiation will spontaneously lead to the nine subjects of the English National Curriculum, which might be seen to support the conclusion that the National Curriculum could be re-presented in less differentiated terms, ones which are more closely aligned with children's perceptions. D. Hargreaves (1991) has developed this theme, arguing that integration between subjects is necessary if the curriculum as a whole is to have coherence.

It is also valuable to recognise that in topic work it is the child who may integrate the subject matter, which may be more powerful than having the teacher provide an integration which appears disjointed to the child. However, the teacher is not redundant. A serendipity curriculum, leaving connections to the child and to chance is not acceptable. Teachers need a view of the possible outcomes of learning and they should make absolutely explicit key concepts, procedures and knowledge, if learning is to be efficient. The psychological view of children's development is not a case for teachers waiting for something to turn up, like Mr Micawber.

## The goals of education

If primary education is principally about helping children to acquire general skills of enquiry and to become thoughtful, then topic work, with its apparent indifference to which particular content the child encounters, is well suited to fostering these general aims. More recently we are told, as a fact and despite the American experience that,

> the cross-curricular themes in particular will involve pupils in active learning and in becoming rational and independent thinkers, able to solve real problems by collecting appropriate data, both independently and in co-operation with others (Craft, 1991, p.184; see also Craft, 1992).

There are two problems with these views of the power of integrated approaches to the curriculum. The first is that however desirable Craft's aims are, their history is not propitious, nor are they necessarily best served by cross-curricular approaches. The second objection does not apply to Craft's position but to an older view that the process of learning far outweighed the product. The counter-argument is that schooling entails the transmission of a culture, a culture which comprises propositional knowledge as well as the procedural knowledge of enquiry and reflection. On that view topic work is acceptable in so far as it is shown to support the efficient teaching of the desired propositions.

Moreover, the critics of topic work point out that procedural knowledge is subject specific; that is to say that skills (procedural knowledge) are not separable from content (propositional knowledge). If that is the case, then there are awkward implications for the claim that topic work is valuable as a way of developing general skills, since the counter claim is that skills are always tied to content.

*Pragmatic – the teacher voice*

Primary teachers have not been used to teaching separate subjects, preferring cross-curricular topic approaches. There is a case for saying that it makes sense to go with the grain of that expertise, not to cut across it, a view implicit in Morgan's approach (1992) to planning geography topics for Key Stage 2.

*Pragmatic – timetabling*

Partly as a means of covering more material efficiently, and partly because it emphasises the reality of the world in which we live, a cross-curricular approach has been emphasised ... in the core curriculum areas of Mathematics, Science and English (Harling, 1990, p.vii).

Generally, history will be taught in a context that is broadly cross-curricular. Paradoxically the heavy demands of a subject-driven National Curriculum may have ensured that subject barriers will have to stay down. Integrating subjects may well be the best way of getting to grips with its heavy subject content (Noble, 1991, p.4).

**Forms of integration**

Even a well-established form of integration, such as American social studies is not free from ambiguities. Leming (1991) identified six main views of social studies which were held by elementary school teachers, namely: social studies is a non-subject; it's about human relationships; about citizenship; it's a form of school knowledge; it comprises the integrative core of the curriculum; it is education for social action. At the other end of the scale is the much looser 'topic work' approach of English primary education, which Burroughs (1988, p.149) described as,

> any set of learning activities which are given an 'umbrella' title such as 'Me' or 'Water' etc. It may include factual accounts, visits, experimental work and research across subject disciplines, imaginative and expressive work ... experienced, under-taken and recorded in a diversity of modes and media.

Falling between these two types of 'integration' are a number of other approaches. Pring (1976) identified four main forms. One involved the correlation of content, so that the geography of another part of the UK which happened to be an area swollen by the Victorian industrial revolution, would be studied alongside the history of Victorian England. This could describe the topic web approach, or work integrated around the study of an area (European or local studies). The second was integration through topics, such as 'me' or 'water', which might be seen as being closely related to the National Curriculum idea of cross-curricular themes. The third element was the integration which follows from practical enquiry, from problem-working. Lastly, came learner-initiated enquiries, of the sort which can constitute individual topic work. Obviously a study may be both learner-initiated and organised around the correlation of content, or it may be a practical enquiry within a topic framework. Furthermore, it is possible for a correlation of content to be 'non-differentiated' (Alexander *et al*, 1992), occurring without any particular thought having gone into what is correlated with what, let alone why. Equally, content might have been painstakingly drawn together on principled grounds. We should also note that different types of integration involve different claims about the likely benefits, with type one (correlation) being easily explained in terms of efficient use of time, whereas type four (learner-initiated) would be associated with ideas of autonomous learning and motivation. Yet, this is a simple and powerful classification, which will be alluded to in the following discussion of integration.

There are four purposes of this review of six approaches to integration. One is to illustrate the importance of having a centre around which to integrate. The second is to show something of the range of possibilities, while the third is to set the discussion of integration in a more definite humanities context than hitherto. Lastly, I want to imply that the problems with integration are, by and large, practical, not principled problems. That does not make them any the less important but it does mean that they are amenable to different ways of trying to solve them.

*Area approaches to integration – the locality*

The locality is the obvious focus for integration, especially since integrated approaches tend to carry with them the rhetoric of activity, investigation and concreteness which is well matched to work in the immediate area. Unsurprisingly, local studies dominate the Key Stage 1 curriculum in England. HMI (1991b, p.1) have seen particular benefits in local work in primary humanities, observing that, 'work based on themes related to the immediate locality of the school was often the most effective in combining elements of history and geography'.

*Area approaches to integration – world studies*

World studies is a less familiar way of integrating subjects which have been separately defined in the English National Curriculum, so it is covered here in some detail.

Hicks directed the *World Studies 8–13 Project* (Fisher and Hicks, 1985; Hicks and Steiner, 1989). Its purpose was to develop 'the knowledge, attitudes and skills which young people need in order to practise social responsibility in a multicultural society and in an interdependent world' (Hicks and Steiner, 1989, p.iv). The project's concern with global matters gives it a strong geographical flavour and there is an emphasis on studying and evaluating the way in which people use their world, and upon the ways in which different areas are interconnected. Four 'broad problems' – key project themes – are taken as indicative of a global crisis, namely environmental damage and the fragility of ecological balances; the issue of economic inequality, especially as seen in the contrast between 'overdevelopment' and underdevelopment; human rights and questions about justice; and peace and conflict, on personal, local and international levels.

The title 'world studies' is a little misleading, because it suggests that children study foreign places to the exclusion of their own surroundings. In fact the project requires children to think about and investigate their area and their country, and compare and contrast it with other parts of the world in order to understand *them* and *us* better. So, a study of the world's forests (Lyle, 1989) involves looking at the pattern of timber imports to Britain, work on the processes and effects of rainforest destruction, which includes a card game, and a woodland walk as a part of the development of the idea of an ecosystem. A topic on gender issues (Steiner and Hicks, 1989) gets children to collect information about the social roles of women and men around them, examining patterns of work, stereotypes and gender in the classroom. Children's experiences are included in it. This work is complemented by comparisons with the patterns in other parts of the world and values issues pervade it all.

The project books reject didacticism and are full of ideas about ways in which children might acquire information through practical, investigative activities. Steiner (1989, p.23) summarised it thus,

> world studies does not stress active learning for its own sake. It is a means for creating a positive learning environment, building group skills and communicating a consistency between values and action, means and ends.

One problem with this project is that links with history, which might have been prominent, are rather tenuous. The links which might be made with design and technology, science, English, and mathematics also have to be made by readers, rather than by the project's writers.

Pike and Selby (1988) oversaw another British world studies project. They list five headings which together define a basic world studies programme, namely,

- perspective consciousness – realising that our view of the world is not shared by all;
- involvement of consciousness – seeing the impact of our actions upon the planet and developing political action skills to bring about change;
- systems consciousness – seeing the world in terms of interrelated systems;
- awareness of the health of the planet;
- process mindedness – realising that learning and personal development are life-long.

Figure 9.1 shows the connections between their four aspects of global education.

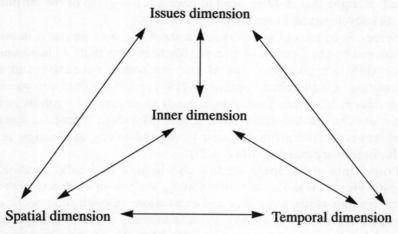

**Figure 9.1:** A model of global studies
**Source:** Selby (1991)

In this model the integration of history with concerns about the future (temporal dimension), geography (spatial dimension) and values (issues dimension) is plainly shown. The 'inner dimension' represents the way that the spatial, issues and temporal dimensions should combine in fostering reflection and self-awareness.

Both projects were primarily campaigns to get a world studies element into the curriculum, making their cases through demonstrations that world studies is a viable school study. The suggested teaching approaches embody many of the more attractive ideas mentioned in Chapters 4, 6 and 8. However, they are not complete humanities or social studies curricula, and they cannot cover much of the material which is required in the English National Curriculum.

*Area approaches to integration – the European dimension*

Between local studies and world studies there are claims that other areas are in some fashion important and worthy of study in their own right. Behind this there is a claim that certain factual knowledge should be taught in schools, since it has some enduring power in adult life. Such claims are more commonly made in respect of the 'basics', where it is often said that children must know their tables or spellings because these are items of knowledge which it is necessary for an adult to have. 'Area studies' advocates seem to emphasise 'awareness' rather than detail, to argue that children need to have a broad grasp of the territory, not an encyclopaedia in memory.

Europe is an area of which children should be well aware, it is said. Sponsored by the Council of Europe, Shennan says that 'a "European" education is a political, social and economic necessity and an affirmation of their cultural birthright' (1991, p.18). 'After twenty years of gestation, European Education is ready to emerge as a robust issue that cannot be brushed aside' (*ibid*, p.200). However, 'Europe is spread over several disciplinary bases [and] the study of Europe is a multidisciplinary exercise' (*ibid*, p.29).

Proponents of European studies also believe that children should develop important skills, such as mapping, analysis of evidence, higher-order reading skills, synthesis and evaluation, through their work on Europe. Obviously, a positive attitude towards a united Europe is a central but far from controversial aim, although indoctrination is not supposed to form any part of their programme.

Yet, if the goals of European studies are otherwise uncontroversial, it is by no means easy to see what European studies should comprise. Perhaps, in England, this is hardly an issue, since in the primary years it is a struggle to lever *any* European work into the mandated curriculum, but in the secondary school it is an issue of some vexatiousness.

Shennan accepted that matters European might be taught through separate subjects, but also considered interdisciplinary arrangements. They might be organised around key concepts, for example 'communism' (a rather battered substantive concept) and 'respect for evidence', a 'European-awareness' and 'open-mindedness' (procedural concepts). This second group of concepts has a high priority in European studies (*ibid*, pp.32, 179) and offers an interesting approach to integration which will be more fully discussed below (p.122).

Shennan thought it important to avoid a 'Euro-myopia' – a European parochialism – and insisted that Europe must be seen in a global context, and that, 'preparation for life in an interdependent world requires subjects like Geography to present European themes and topics, whenever appropriate, within a global context' (*ibid*, p.69).

Although global educators and those interested in Europe may differ in their beliefs about what content should take priority, they appear to share similar procedural values, which permits the conclusion that 'the global and European approaches should be mutually reinforcing' (Shennan, 1991, p.175). Bell (1991, p.110) endorses this position.

Unfortunately, neither writer addressed the complex pedagogical issues which go with the stance that primary school children should develop global, European, national and local perspectives.

As with world studies, the pedagogy is important. This is partly based on the belief that if a goal is to encourage critical enquiry so that children develop soundly based attitudes and awarenesses, then the teaching should not take a didactic and prescriptive approach. It is partly based on theories about effective teaching and learning approaches in the humanities. Hence both Bell and Shennan discuss teaching methods, not as an appendix of teaching hints, but because they see the methods as inseparable from the matter.

In several respects their position challenges the traditional topic work which has been done in British schools. Cross-curricular it may have been but, it was often resource led and dominated by information gathering: 'if you let children work freely in this kind of teaching they are mainly going to collect nice pictures, travel brochures etc.' (Dutch teacher, quoted in Bell, 1991, p.45). Writing of 'the limitations of resource-based teaching', Bell added (*ibid*, p.104),

> the tendency here may be to be too reliant on the materials made available at the expense of the reflection necessary for teachers to clarify their own knowledge skills and attitudes towards a concept of Europe ... This ... applies equally to pupils. They too need to be encouraged to hypothesise, ... to visualise ... to suppose and to materialise ideas.

European – and world – studies demand that the teacher is clear about the processes and the awarenesses which are to be at the centre of the work. *Laissez-faire* approaches, in the name of encouraging pupil autonomy, cannot deliver what the proponents of these area approaches promise. In Bell's words, reflecting Alexander (1984),

> critical reflection will certainly be required on old habits if the European dimension is to be realised. Critical attention in particular will have to be paid to the weaknesses as much as the strengths of child-centred theory, the management of topic and project work ... and not least the pedagogy of controversial issues including the vexed issue of the quality of the global environment (1991, pp.84–5).

Area studies approaches, be they global, local, Pacific or European in scale, require integration at least in the sense of curriculum co-ordination, which implies a shared sense of purpose and pace. However, they do not solve the problems of integration and the endemic problems of balance, coherence and progression are in no way banished. Area studies offer a way of organising a part of the curriculum, but they are not a neat solution to the difficulties which have beset primary humanities: arguably, they make for a more complex curriculum and increase the demands on teachers whose first task is to be seen to follow the subject-specific National Curriculum.

*Thematic approaches to integration – the environment*

Thematic approaches are within Pring's second category of integration, integration around a topic or a theme, although they are also closely associated with the concept of integration as a practical enquiry, since themes such as environmental education often comprise bunches of problems in need of 'solutions'. It is hard to see how simple co-ordination of separate subjects could do much to advance this sort of integration, since it is necessary to have some grasp of the nature of the problems and of the concerns and concepts which lie at the heart of the theme. There is no reason why, having identified these central elements, they should not be disaggregated and then built into individual subjects, so that the cross-curricular theme is taught at many points in the curriculum, overtly or covertly. The point is that the theme first needs to be understood, analysed and worked out before it can be parcelled out amongst subjects. Even then, there will probably be 'leftovers', elements which do not neatly fit within the National Curriculum programmes of study,[2] and there will also be a need to spend some time in drawing together the concepts and awarenesses which have been separately developed.

The alternative is to teach a theme, such as environmental studies, separately, using prescribed programmes of study to provide the bulk of the content. This too has drawbacks, but it and the subject-centred approach are both superior to the non-differentiated approach, where environmental education is ruined by unawareness of its central concerns and a lack of understanding of how art, geography, history and science must contribute to work on these concerns.

Shennan said that it is helpful to teach children *about* Europe (essentially factual), *through* Europe (promotion of general abilities) and *for* Europe (developing values concepts). A similar point has become commonplace in discussions of environmental education (Huckle, 1990; NCC, 1990a), although growing awareness of the harmful impact people are making on the ecosystem means that perhaps education *for*

2 The National Curriculum is only the basic curriculum and schools are expected to provide more besides, a point which has often been overlooked in the panic to keep afloat in the ever-changing sea of basics.

the environment should be paramount, a view which is implicit in Pike and Selby's (1988) stance that world studies should develop awareness of the health of the planet.

Huckle's view of the aims of environmental education was designed for high schools, but seems to be broadly adaptable to primaries too (1990, pp.158-9).

- Knowledge of the natural environment and its potential for human use;
- A theoretical and practical grasp of appropriate technology;
- A sense of history and knowledge of the impact of changing social formations on the environment;
- An awareness of class conflict;
- Political literacy;
- An awareness of alternative social and environmental futures;
- An understanding of environmental ideology and consumer lifestyles;
- Involvement in real issues;
- Balance;
- Optimism. If we are not to overwhelm pupils with the world's problems, we should teach in a spirit of optimism.

So broad is the area Huckle has staked out that it is tantamount to a description of education itself (Gayford, 1991). Yet, at the same time, environmental education is an area inhabited by many single-issue pressure groups, concerned to improve air quality, to preserve birds, to stop litter pollution, to obstruct *this* development or to preserve *that* vestige of the past. Consequently, it is not easy for teachers to strive for a coherent, recurring form of integration around the global environmental theme which embodies a progression of understanding, skills and knowledge, and which is sensitive to the health of the planet. In England, official guidance (NCC, 1990a) has been characterised as posing more problems than it solves, which leaves the teacher torn between tokenism (a coping strategy), and trying to sort the bits and pieces out herself, probably in the knowledge that her efforts will be less well regarded than if they had been directed towards mathematics learning. An unfortunate consequence may be a 'return to the worst horrors of interdisciplinarity when the chemistry of water was studied in science while in religious education children learnt about Moses parting the Red Sea' (Hawkins, 1990/1, p.5).

The complexity of some thematic approaches may prove their

undoing.

*Approaches to integration – citizenship*

Education for good citizenship is often seen as the major goal of American social studies (Brophy, 1990a) and is something to be fostered by the English curriculum. Citizenship may amount to dreary civics, but it may also embrace concerns with the environment and the locality; with Europe and the wider world.

Guidance from the English government (NCC, 1990b) has depicted citizenship education as an activity in which children participate, discuss, form moral codes and values, and acquire positive attitudes:

> Education for citizenship develops the knowledge, skills and attitudes necessary for exploring, making informed judgements and exercising rights and responsibilities in a democratic society (NCC, 1990b, p.2).

Some content knowledge is specified, although it is rather general, in Key Stage 1 amounting to the sort of work on the community which would naturally be subsumed under local studies and to general personal and social education. In Key Stage 2 links are made with history to show, for example, that Britain is a nation composed of many different sets of migrants and to show how societies are law governed; with geography, so that children investigate patterns of leisure and work; and with RE, notably in the context of considering what counts as moral behaviour.

This content appears fragmented, hardly the stuff of a strong integrating force in the curriculum. It is easy to see how such general ideas and dispositions might readily be taught as a normal, natural and necessary part of world or European studies. It is hard to see that it needs separate attention, let alone that it could serve as a theme which would stand alone. Ironically, the less demanding a cross-curricular theme, the less power it has to act as a centre around which elements of the curriculum might be integrated.

*Non-differentiation as integration – the topic web approach*

This has been the commonest approach to integration in England. A theme is selected, such as 'water' and through a process which can best be described as free association, content links are made with as many curriculum areas as the planner has a taste for. So, the water topic might look as shown in Figure 9.2.

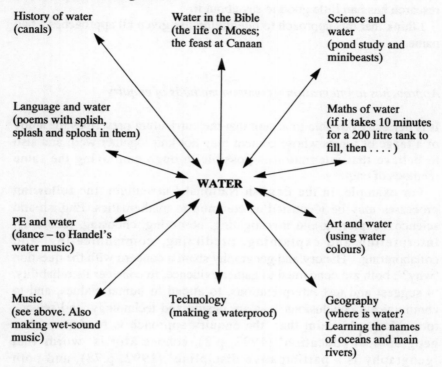

History of water
(canals)

Water in the Bible
(the life of Moses;
the feast at Canaan

Science and
water
(pond study and
minibeasts)

Language and water
(poems with splish,
splash and splosh in them)

Maths of water
(if it takes 10 minutes
for a 200 litre tank to
fill, then . . . . )

**WATER**

PE and water
(dance – to Handel's
water music)

Art and water
(using water
colours)

Music
(see above. Also
making wet-sound
music)

Technology
(making a waterproof)

Geography
(where is water?
Learning the names
of oceans and main
rivers)

**Figure 9.2:** A view of the topic-web approach to integration

This approach produced some forced links, and we must wonder whether the coherence which the teacher may have thought had been achieved ever communicated itself to children. Pring (1976, p.107) considered this to be

> nothing more than the idiosyncratic association of ideas of one particular teacher ... many examples of integrated curricula ... have frequently substituted an individual's structuring of reality ... for a socially developed mode of thinking which has already been found adequate and has withstood scrutiny by others.

This conflicts with the claim which is often made that children must be allowed to construct their own meanings, the irony being not so much that this sort of quixotic integration impedes that process, but rather that it replaces the public meanings of established subjects with the teacher's individual association of materials. Perhaps this is caricaturing an approach which led to some interesting projects, but then research has had little good to say about it.

I think that this approach to integration has given all approaches a bad name.

## *Approaches to integration – common methods of enquiry*

It is perfectly possible to accept that the curriculum prescribes the study of a range of topics whose content may not knit together well, and also to believe that integration is possible through employing the same methods of enquiry.

For example, in the English National Curriculum, the following processes may be identified as common to mathematics, English and science: exploring and investigating, observing, choosing, recording, interpreting and explaining, predicting, communicating, and collaborating. History and geography share a concern with the question 'why?': both are concerned to gather evidence, to consider its reliability, to suggest and test interpretations, to attend to human values, and to communicate conclusions – as are design and technology, and science too. Morgan's claim that 'the enquiry approach is fundamental to geographical education' (1992, p.2), echoes Morris' words that 'geography is a participative discipline' (1992, p.78), and both comments would apply as well to science, technology, English, art ..., as to geography.

There is, then, the possibility of reinforcing similar rules of procedure and of promoting similar metacognition through work on sharply separated contents. As we saw in Chapters 3 and 4, there is some optimism that these strategies will be educationally productive. However, if ever an approach to integration demanded a whole-school approach, this is it, which returns us to Chapter 2.

## Drawbacks to integration

This is not a repetition of the criticisms listed above, but rather an attempt to highlight points relating to the specific approaches which have been discussed above.

● These themes are either not supported by published resources or publishers, faced with marketing dilemmas, have adopted anodyne solutions.

● In England official guidance (where it exists) is of little value, since it beckons teachers to play a game of 'checklists' in which they search existing topics, like inquisitors hunting for evidence of witchcraft, looking for hints of environmental education, of economic awareness, of citizenship education and so on. Like the Witchfinder General, they find the evidence. Whether the children also find it is another, very different question.

● Each approach makes considerable demands upon the teacher's mental and professional energies. It is a fierce intellectual challenge to build cross-curricular coherence out of the bag of bits which is the National Curriculum. In normal, day-to-day primary practice teachers find it hard to live up to their educational ideals (Desforges and Cockburn, 1987; Alexander *et al*, 1992), as a consequence of insufficient planning, underdeveloped management skills, a lack of technical knowledge, or of unawareness of what they actually do. The more complex the classroom task is made – and integration does complicate a curriculum written in subject-specific terms – the harder it is for teachers to live up to the ideals.

● No-one gets ahead by investing in the frills, rather than in the core subjects. Current emphases on measurement and testing work against those forms of integration which centre upon values rather than upon any particular body of knowledge, while the low status of any save the core subjects means that the time does not appear to be available to develop nor to teach about these areas.

## Integration as immanent in geography and history

One stance is that, irrespective of whether it is desirable to integrate subjects or not, some integration of geography and history is, in fact, inevitable since both subjects take humanity as their subjects and, in consequence, span all human knowledge. The one is especially interested in the variations in space, the other with variations over human time. Doing geography or history is, by definition, an act of subject integration. This approaches Pring's first category of integration, the co-ordination of subjects, although in this case the co-ordination takes place within the study of geography or history.

Dewey, writing in 1899, went further. 'Geography', he said, 'loses much of its meaning when separated from history and history loses a good deal of its content if you isolate it entirely from geography' (cit Kleibard, 1986, p.64). Far from it being the case that the criticisms of integrated approaches founder when it comes to considering some alliance between geography and history, it appears that sharing a common subject – people – means that there is a good case for considering them as bedfellows. But then, cases have been seen, such as Hartshorne's, for keeping them apart and given the disjunctions of the National Curriculum – disjunctions not absent from the integrated Scottish National Curriculum either – it is easy to see how they may, in practice, be separated.

## Integrated humanities? A summary

Integration in English primary schools has enjoyed much support and little success: plentiful problems have been seen, many of them re-statements of points recorded in earlier chapters.

Is the idea of joining history and geography together a futile one?

It will be argued that it is not. Most of the criticisms of integration have either been political (that the humanities lack a tradition, an academic reference point and a cadre of supporters), or practical (that the aims have not been fulfilled in international practice). The political claims will not be resolved by the exercise of reason or evidence, but by power and fashion, and so they are laid to one side for political attention. As for the practical objections to integration, the international story of disappointment should make us properly cautious about assuming that things might be done better. Nevertheless, it is worth considering integration seriously because practical problems may be soluble, particularly now that the national curricula introduced in the UK have removed one source of these problems by prescribing minimum goals and content coverage. Four reasons for some integration of history and geography are suggested below:

- history and geography are both concerned with the same subjects – people;
- national curricula give history and geography common topics to study – notably the locality, which is also covered by other subjects;
- the humanities share many processes of enquiry with each other and with other studies too;

- the practicalities of fitting nine subjects plus cross-curricular themes and other appurtenances of a balanced and broadly based curriculum into the primary school week demand that two subjects are frequently taught simultaneously. Barnes (1989), writing of art was clear on this: 'Only when we fail to see the relationship between art and the rest of the curriculum does there seem to be a serious problem regarding the allocation of time for art' (p.4).

To repeat a point, though: the promise depends on realistic integration, on separate subject teaching where necessary, on clarity of goals, on collaboration and agreement amongst a school's staff, and on shared ways of working: a formidable set of pre-requisites. With that in mind, the question arises of what this might look like in practice. That is the subject of the next chapter.

## Chapter 10

# *Re-integrating the Primary Curriculum*

On practical, ideological, epistemological and historical grounds there is a case for a measure of subject integration in the primary curriculum. However, neither in the form of social studies, nor in the hazier shape of topic or project work, has subject integration in the humanities been without its critics. It has been asserted that the English National Curriculum, written in terms of single subjects, may, nevertheless be re-integrated to some degree. This needs to be substantiated, which requires us to consider the organisational issues, for the history of curriculum innovation is full of bold experiments which could be made to work on paper, in the lecture theatre or by the devoted teacher, but which failed to hold their own in the hurly-burly of life in normal classrooms.

The analytical categories suggested by Pring which were used in the last chapter will now be supplanted by another way of classifying approaches to integration. Four forms of integration will be considered, as shown in Figure 10.1:

| Integration of | | |
|---|---|---|
| By content. | 1. History and geography. | 4. Humanities and other subjects. |
| By process. | 2. Humanities concepts and procedures. | 3. Cross-curricular concepts and metacognition. |

**Figure 10.1:** Modes of subject integration for the humanities

In Figure 10.1 the top row approximates to Pring's group 1, and possibly to his group 2 as well, while the bottom row contains his group 3 and possibly group 4 too. It is worth recalling that content and process are not clearly separate categories, and that subjects might be integrated through the content *and* through the methods. For the sake of completeness, the cross-curricular themes of the English National Curriculum will be treated as a fifth type of integration.

### Geography and history – integration through content

In Key Stage 1 the geography curriculum is centred upon the locality, although there is a vague requirement that children should notice other countries too. The history curriculum is dominated by history within living memory. This could mean that children in Birmingham find out about how their recent ancestors came to England and to the Midlands, but the locality in which they now live would undeniably be at the heart of the study. The historical fact that children's families will have come from many different places is a useful introduction to the important geographical themes of movement, settlement and location. Simple map work is invited by this topic. However, the history curriculum for Key Stage 1 also requires children to hear stories of famous men and women, who will not, in the main, be local. They should also study a patch of the more distant past, which could indeed be locally based, but which need not be (Knight, 1992).

But basically, it may be said that history and geography at this level are joined by a concern with the same area, quite literally. The historian's interest in how it used to be in the recent past, and in how it changed, is complemented by the geographer's interest in describing where things are, why and how the space of the locality is used: complementary questions about the same space. There is no reason for disintegrating the infant curriculum, as long as the distinctive concerns of the two disciplines are present throughout the enquiries.

At Key Stage 2 things are more complicated, since the geography curriculum continues to require a study of the locality and its 'home region' (whatever that is), which is to be contrasted with a locality elsewhere in the UK. A study of a locality in a developing country is also required, and children working towards level 5 may work on a country in the European Community (which is desirable on many grounds), although in the interests of organisational simplicity it is likely that they will wait until secondary school to become Europeans. A gazetteer of place names is to be learnt and children should be able to place the names on standard maps. There is no such requirement for

Scottish children, although this detailed factual knowledge has some appeal in parts of the USA.

As we have seen, history content is also specified in some detail. Four of the nine topics are on national history, although it is expected that children will relate the national to the local wherever possible, so Cumbrian children will acknowledge the Viking past when studying 'Invaders and settlers'. So, there is some scope here for a history/geography link around the theme of the locality, but it has to be said that if the locality is encountered only as a set of examples to enliven the (rather disjointed) national story, then there is a grave danger of forced and sterile links being perpetuated.

Schools, though, are obliged to develop at least one local history study unit. The school which cannot tailor a history unit to enrich and support the geography work is either very short of imagination or rightly queasy about repeating Key Stage 1 work. This fear may be eased by holding the Key Stage 2 local study unit off until Y6, which can also be justified on the grounds that schools have to help children to become more independent in their history learning, which can admirably culminate in a local study topic in which they apply the strategies learned through the other topics to a field rich in accessible primary and secondary sources. It is the older children's ability to use a wider range of sources and to apply level 4 rather than level 2 concepts which should reduce the Key Stage 1/Key Stage 2 overlap.

In the history curriculum, one study in development must be chosen. While some, such as 'writing and printing' could only be joined with geography through forced links, 'houses and places of worship' could open up questions about location and migration, as well as physical geography when building materials are considered. More promising are 'food and farming', 'ships and seafarers' and 'land transport'. Here the danger is almost that the vibrant geographical concepts could overwhelm the history, which could emerge simply as a dull list of developments (cf Knight, 1991b, pp.8–9).

Other topics are less promising. Children must study 'ancient Greece' (a rather awkward link with geography *at level 5 only* might be made here), 'explorations and encounters c1450 – c1550', and one of six non-Western civilisations. The most vigorous link with geography might come through the need to study a locality within a developing country, particularly since there is a strongly held view that it was Western imperialism, beginning with the explorations of the sixteenth century, which is the cause of many of the developing countries' current problems. Mexico could be chosen to provide a locality in a developing country, which could then be woven in with the story of the Spanish *conquistadores'* capture of Mexico and of their transformation of its economy and genocidal religious customs. As a developing country, Mexico well illustrates the paradoxes of advancement and desperation, of inequalities, of inappropriate solutions which are themselves part of the problems, and of the way in which environmental well-being is sacrificed to the need to try to keep things from getting even worse: Mexico City provides a spectacular locale in which to set these issues.[3]

In terms of organising the history aspect as a school topic, key ideas include: the power and achievements of the Aztecs, which necessarily means looking at where they lived and what the place was like – both naturally and as a result of their actions; the motives of Cortes and his crew, and the reasons why they, completely against the odds, lived, never mind why they conquered; the effects of the conquest, seen from different points of view.

This section will not be strongly rooted in work on primary sources, which are sparse and which have the irritating habit of being in Spanish or in Aztec glyphs. Notions of change (HAT1a, levels 3–5), of cause and consequence (HAT1b, levels 2–5) and of interpretation (HAT2, especially levels 2 and 4) could dominate this history-led part of the topic. Map recognition and use will be practised. It does not seem to me to be too fruitful to try to force GAT3 (physical geography), GAT4 (human geography), and GAT5 (environmental geography) into *this part* of the topic. Since GAT2 is essentially about knowledge of local places, there is little scope for that either. At this point in the topic integration takes the form of allowing one subject to lead, while the other lurks in the wings.

The same is true for the study of a locality in modern Mexico. Work should be done on HAT1a, change between the mid-sixteenth and the late-twentieth century, and the comparison needs to be extended to one between Mexico and England today. The spirit of HAT2 should also alert children to the different interpretations of the way Mexico is today, with the haves seeing things differently from the have nots, with town and country also diverging. However, it is geography which will dominate at this stage of the topic. The non-statutory guidance for geography (NCC, 1991a, pp.C6, 7) suggests that children will look at features of the area, including physical features, and their impact on people's lives, recognising that jobs and wealth distribution will play their part in shaping lifestyles. Comparison between there (Mexico) and here is encouraged, and children are also to look at recent or proposed changes. Morgan (1992) is more explicit about the features which

3 Fuller notes on Mexico are available from the author on receipt of a stamped, addressed envelope.

might be covered, including details of diet, clothing and housing; of religion, work, schooling and trade; of leisure activities and patterns of movement generally; of different people's views; and so on. Through comparison of there and here,

> opportunities arise ... for discovery of the shared human need for shelter, sustenance and clothing, and of the universality of work, whether in terms of subsistence, manufacture, service or trade. Children will be introduced to the reality of life in another place, avoiding the extremes of the picturesque or repugnant view of distant places (p.6).

Perhaps wishfully, she adds that 'a positive attitude towards people far away should result'.

It is important to insist that simply because it is possible to integrate history and geography around the twin themes of ancient civilisations (history) and a locality in a developing nation (geography) it does not follow that it is necessarily the best way to choose which topics to do. Arguably, there are more important developing nations than Egypt, Iraq, Nigeria, Mexico or India. The purpose of this section is to show possibilities, not to constrain decision-making.

## History and geography – integration through process

'Process' is loosely understood as 'ways of working' and includes procedural concepts such as causation, change, similarity and difference. There is some artificiality in this separation of content and process, but it is a useful analytical device.

The history ATs imply that children will learn certain ways of working, appreciating that a range of sources can be put together to produce a picture of the past (HAT3) and that different pictures can be drawn, partly because the sources disagree with one another, and partly because different interpretations are possible (HAT2). The programme of study for Key Stage 2 makes this explicit, requiring that children,

> should be helped to investigate historical topics on their own. They should be shown how to organise and communicate historical information in a variety of ways. They should have opportunities to ask questions, choose sources for an investigation, collect and record information ... select and organise historical information ... present results orally, visually and in writing (DES, 1991c, p.17).

There is no ringing statement in the geography curriculum about the importance of certain modes of enquiry, the nearest being that

> enquiry should form an important part of pupils' work in Key Stage 2. It should take account of pupils' interests, experience and capabilities and lead to investigation based on fieldwork (DES, 1991b, p.35).

However, scrutiny shows that the geography attainment targets involve children in collecting data (about the weather (GAT1), about the locality (GAT2), about settlement patterns (GAT4), and about the environment in general (GAT5). In Key Stage 2 they will be using the contents and index sections of atlases (DES, 1991b, p.35), and using a wide range of sources (GAT3 level 4), from which they select the most appropriate data for their purposes (*ibid;* NCC, 1991a, p.C24). They should raise questions (GAT4), make suggestions (GAT5, level 3) and take action (GAT5, level 2). Implicit in making suggestions and identifying reasons is the notion of interpretation, and where teachers allow values issues to come to the fore, especially in respect of environmental and human geography, these interpretations will loom as large as they do in history, even though they do not have the benefit of a separate AT. Needless to say, children will produce descriptions of places as a way of communicating some of the findings of their investigations in the same varied range of ways as they will produce descriptions of different times (DES, 1991c, p.17). The similarities in process, cloaked though they are by the documents, are apparent, and the differences are ones to do with the different sources of information used in the two subjects.

Both history and geography share interests in cause and effect (GAT4, HAT1b), and both are concerned with change and continuity (HAT1a, GAT2, 4, 5). In geography, surveys and interviews can be rather more used than in history, while historical sources can have their own peculiarities. Maps are more central to geography than history, and there is more of a tradition of geographical fieldwork too. However, the differences in process seem trivial compared to the similarities. This may be clearly seen in the Scottish proposals for environmental studies which have a separate Attainment Outcome called 'investigating', which describes five processes which are common to science, geography and history, namely, planning, finding out, recording, interpreting and reporting (Scottish Office, 1992). The list may have the air of a lowest common denominator about it, but it is a useful pointer to the common process of enquiry which unites history and geography.

If this integration of process is to be effective it is important for schools (not individual teachers) to be very clear about what they wish to teach the children to do. In a nutshell, they need to identify key enquiry strategies, to teach them deliberately and to make sure that children are aware of the range of enquiry strategies which they are acquiring, which is – to labour a point – a manifestation of metacognition. Without this children may be engaged in enquiry but learn nothing about enquiring, except as an accidental by-product of their work. Hence, the task of formulating a whole-school policy for the processes of enquiry in history and geography is not a trivial, nor a simple matter: but then that is a quintessential point about integration.

## The humanities and other subjects – integration by process

The last section reviewed some of the ways of working common to history and geography. It is apparent that these procedures are shared with science, art, some forms of drama, some activities in English, and with practical, problem-working mathematics. There are, of course, differences. Yet, there is a surprising robustness about the science concept of a fair test – that is the concept of posing a question, imagining a way of finding out what the answer might be, and then fairly collecting evidence to test the answer – for such modes of enquiry are as characteristic of history and geography as they are of science. In geography we might wonder whether hypermarkets are often built in similar sorts of place, and in history we might suppose that few Victorians lived past the age of 40. Both questions may be subjected to fair tests, the difference between this and science being in the sort of material which can be used as evidence, not in the basic rules of enquiry.

This takes us back into territory which was explored in Chapter 4, in which the issue was raised of whether intellectual development is general or domain specific in character. The general 'thinking' programmes associated with Lipman, Feuerstein and DeBono endorse the general development stance, encouraging children, in Feuerstein's case, to look for relationships and patterns, to categorise, compare, analyse, plan and reflect. Lipman's 'philosophy for children' uses group discussion methods to explore the moral dilemmas which are nested in especially written materials, thereby fostering exactly the sort of reasoning and enquiry skills which are so important in the humanities. However, a common weakness of these programmes has been that there have not been enough opportunities for this general reasoning to be applied to the regular curriculum, so perhaps it is not surprising that studies of the programmes' effects have not consistently shown that any gains are transferred to mainstream curriculum subjects. That, of course, could be a problem with the mainstream curriculum. Evidence from the Oxfordshire Skills Project (Craft, 1991, p.193) has shown that 'the transfer of skill depends on a common language being available for problem-solving or thinking across subjects'. In other words, it may be that a major obstacle to integration around the processes of enquiry is that insufficient attention has been paid to making this a consistent, regular *whole curriculum* initiative, with the result that children have not learned – or been taught – to apply what they know to a variety of contexts and situations over a period of several years. They have not, quite simply, routinised the application of their thinking skills.

The special cases of English and mathematics need attention here. Both the Bullock Report on English, and the Cockcroft Report on mathematics, said that these were subjects which should cross the curriculum: reading and writing were to be the concerns of all teachers, and mathematics was to be used as an everyday tool for problem working.

In reading, for example, children at level 3 are expected to use reference books in order to answer questions; to use catalogues (level 4); to use indices, contents pages, sub-headings and the like to locate information (level 5); and to make inferences and deductions about text (level 4), particularly in identifying the difference between fact and opinion (level 5). The National Writing Project (1989) has demonstrated the power of cross-curricular work for enhancing children's writing, and the National Curriculum requires children to revise, redraft and produce a variety on non-chronological writing (level 3); to pay attention to organisational concerns (level 4); and to write in a way appropriate to an audience. Similar points can be made about spelling (which the Bullock Committee saw as best learned in a context, for a purpose), and speaking and listening (which is, of course a fundamental part of humanities work).

Not only are these English requirements ones which may be met through humanities work, but also, far more importantly, they are ones which *should* be deliberately fostered in the varied and life-like setting of humanities (and science and technology) work. If that is not done, there is not just a danger of curriculum overload, but there is also a definite danger that children will be taught the principles of language but be deprived of important opportunities to apply, refine and extend those principles so that they become tools of learning, not just objects of learning.

The position with mathematics is similar, but as far as the humanities are concerned the natural links are less pronounced, being most obvious in the areas of using mathematics to work on some real-life problems; data collection, processing and interpretation; and scale, direction and co-ordinates. Yet this is not an insubstantial, nor an insignificant list.

But, to repeat a key point, integration by process demands a whole-school and a whole-curriculum approach in which the most determined efforts are made to encourage metacognition and the spontaneous transfer of learning from *this* context to *that*.

## Integration by content – the humanities and other subjects

Doubtless history and geography, or history or geography, can be joined in terms of content with other subjects. Art, science and music are obvious examples. Yet more is not always better. It has been argued (Mortimore *et al*, 1988) that topics which embraced several subjects were less effective than those which concentrated on two, or at most three. Presumably, the more ambitious the range, the more the teacher needs to keep in mind in order to get it effectively covered. In busy classrooms, where routines are at a premium, it often proves impossible to juggle too many aims at once, and so the lowest common denominator prevails.

Perhaps influenced by this, a number of commentators have turned towards the idea of integration around a subject core. Cooper (1992) has described topics on the Tudors, the Greeks and history within living memory which incorporate worthwhile mathematical, musical, technological, English and scientific activities too. These activities are clearly subordinate to the history focus, although they are not trivial, representing as they do material which is required by the English National Curriculum.

Morgan (1992) took a similar line with geography, describing topics which are geography focused but which can be enriched by work on history, technology, information technology and mathematics.

The position seems to me to be well summed up by Barnes (1989), who approached integration with art as his starting point. He insisted that the integrity of art must be paramount when considering whether it should be taught within a topic or separately, and paid particular attention to the way that a topic setting could lead to 'art' being stripped of its quintessential creative vision and rendered down into a method of recording information – or of filling in time and space in exercise books. Furthermore, he was sure that children needed to learn, make mistakes with, discover and practise a range of techniques and ways of seeing.

Yet, committed to the specialness of art, he argued that worthwhile art work could be done within a topic work setting, so that a topic on the Victorians need not lead to the sterile re-drawing of pictures of Victorian life, but could more profitably produce a whole series of stimuli to artistic engagement, asking children,

> how many different ways could you use any shape drawn from a Victorian railway station? ... Make a drawing of a part of a Victorian building or a Victorian costume and spend a couple of days fiddling with detail like cracks in stonework ... shoes ... the detail on fabrics ... make rubbings from surfaces, compare, contrast and use for collage (pp.89–90).

On the Vikings, he rejects using art 'as factual illustration' (p.82), sketches of Viking objects and claims that

> artistic concerns, however, are more those linking 'The Vikings' with mood, feeling, emotion, colour, line, form, texture, shape, pattern, design, and so on. Above all *interpretation* is a necessary feature of any creative artwork (*ibid*).

The conclusion is simple and powerful. Where the teacher is clear about the distinctive essence of a subject, then she is well placed to consider whether it can be developed by integration or whether it might be compromised in the process. However confident the teacher is, there is good reason to think that less is more, that it is better to join a couple of subjects together than to try to form a host.

The humanities will often be integrated with other subjects, but not always. Writing of geography, Morgan (1992) identified 'earthquakes and volcanoes' as material which was best covered by a concise geography topic, treated separately. Such a pragmatic approach to integration may help us to avoid the failure of practice to match ambition which has been partly caused by having the unreasonable ambition of integrating everything with anything.

## Integration and cross-curricular themes

The strategy of planning for integration by beginning with a cross-curricular theme such as 'environmental education', is fundamentally different from the approaches discussed above: where they begin with the subjects and look for strong similarities, this approach tries to fit subjects into themes. At its worst this can reproduce the topic webs which were mocked in the previous chapter, and in the past the criticisms of triviality and eccentricity were often valid. In England now this thematic approach is vulnerable to the charge that it fails to guarantee proper subject coverage and that gaps can be left where aspects of the programmes of study have not been attended to. Nevertheless, there is an intellectual case for planning a curriculum by *starting* with the cross-curricular themes and then worrying about which aspects of the subject prescriptions have not been covered.

As an indication that the approach might be viable, consider how environmental education might be associated with the history curriculum at Key Stage 2. History has been chosen rather than geography since although history has a powerful contribution to make to environmental education, geography and science are more usually identified as its natural parents.

It is necessary to start by wrestling with the question of what environmental education is. It is helpful to follow the definition endorsed by the National Association for Environmental Education (NAEE):

> Environmental education is the process of recognising values and clarifying concepts in order to develop skills and attitudes necessary to understand and appreciate the inter-relatedness amongst people, their culture and biological and physical surroundings. Environmental education also entails practice in decision making and self formulation of a code of behaviour about issues concerning environmental quality (NAEE, 1992).

Before proceeding to examine this history-environment dialectic, it is helpful to recall that primary history is about how people made it so that things got to be as they are – how the Lake District got to be sheep ranch, the Weald of Kent to be arable country, and how Milton Keynes got to exist at all. It involves asking this 'why' question about states of affairs, about people's habitual ways of life – why did the Tudors live like that? How did they use and modify their physical environment, and with what results? Why did so many people die so young (an environmental education question if ever there was one)? What changed? For the better? For whom?

It is not the case that history needs environmental education, for history necessarily involves it. Unless children are asking those sort of questions about past times which might be called 'environmental' questions, they are not doing history properly, but they may also regularly be asking these questions in history without ever being made to stand back and see that they have also been learning about people and their environments. This is a recurrent theme of this book, that it is not sufficient to do or to know something: teachers and children need to become aware that they know or have done it.

There are four main senses in which environmental studies ideas should be present in any history study unit.

- People's lives, at any time, have been *in part* the product of a balance between technology and the environment. Obviously beliefs, culture, social organisation have also been important.
- History is about change (AT1a), not least about change in this pattern of interaction.
- History is about points of view (AT2), not least points of view about the costs and benefits of these changes, from the point of view of different people (rich, poor; men, women; urban, rural) at different times.
- The past is about the present: doing history involves comparing now and then, looking for similarities and differences. And comparing now with then invites us to look to the future as well.

Two examples show how this might work out in practice.

*The Victorians*

From a perspective of change, the children will have used a variety of sources to build up an idea of how England altered over a life-time – perhaps between 1851, the year of the Great Exhibition, and 1903, the year of Victoria's death. This will be done from a series of points of view – those of the rich and poor, of men and women, of townspeople and countryfolk.

An environmental audit might overlay this valuable history work. By referring back to the four key ideas, we may identify a set of questions for children to consider, for example:

- How had the environment been changed over this period? (Principally by urbanisation and manufacturing)

- How had different people's lives been changed?   (Here some children might concentrate on men, others on women, some on towns, others on the countryside.)
- Was this change for the better, or not?  And from whose point of view?
- In environmental terms, how does 1903 compare to 1993?  Has progress been made?  From whose point of view?  At what price – and with what benefits?

It might be important to develop a response to any of these questions through case studies – of public health, of the appearance of an area, of leisure facilities and such like.

Challenging questions, but given the groundwork that has been done, and given a commitment to history as an argumentative study, based upon evidence, one might expect most Key Stage 2 children to be able to engage with these issues at some level.

*Food and farming*

The same format can be adopted for the study of change over the past 100 years, although with this particular topic the trade off between the need to feed people, and the impact upon the environment is always going to be at the fore.  Another key idea is that people have always changed the environment to get their food.

It is suggested that in doing the topic the children should concentrate upon several patches of the past, and infer the story of change by comparing these patches (Knight, 1991b).  At each point they can be asked how the pursuit of food affected the environment (by deforestation, in the sixteenth century).  An interesting question is whether the impact mattered.  Certainly, there were Tudor people who lamented the way that sheep farming was transforming the countryside, but when we consider how it was being changed, it is clear that the level of impact was quite different from the impact that excessive fertiliser use has today.  And then, as now, opinions differed.  So, the environmental audit is a cost-benefit analysis, based upon the evidence of the children's work on patches of the past.  In the process, they encounter points of view, explore notions of change and develop a perspective in which to see the present.

Building environmental issues into mainstream history topics is not only a form of integration which is good for environmental issues, but it also ensures that important history concerns are raised. It becomes possible to see how a planning strategy which began with environmental education, to take one of the cross-curricular themes, and which looked to develop its key concerns through the content laid down in the National Curriculum, could lead to an integrated area of the curriculum in which a great deal of the required history, geography, science, English, mathematics and art could be covered, albeit not all at once.

## Conclusion

The test of integration is not the plausibility of the case for integrating, but the quality of the practice of integration. While the two are not entirely separate, in the past the problem has often been more with the practice than with the theories.

Since the theories differ in the forms of integration which they identify, and in the purposes which they have, it is not surprising that different forms of practice can be described. Some of the forms are far easier to adopt than others, with form 1 (a co-ordination of history and geography content, where appropriate and often through local studies) being much easier for the individual teacher to achieve than form 3 (the integration of processes of enquiry across the curriculum). Notice that even form 1 is markedly different from integrated approaches of yesteryear, since it is now necessary for children to gain and master some propositional knowledge, that is to say that they must know some historical and geographical information and know something about the workings of these subjects. Consequently, the old line which said that topic work could be justified simply for helping children to learn how to learn is no longer good enough.

One of the powerful ideas associated with Total Quality Management (Oakland, 1989), which is gaining ground in the education sector, is that quality may be defined as 'fitness for the purpose'. On that view, quality in the curriculum will partly involve the form of organisation being fitted to the educational purpose, with the implication that there will be points at which a cross-curricular approach is desirable and points where it would be quite inappropriate. It is not, I believe, possible to say either that separate subject teaching is desirable, nor the contrary. Ideology should yield to the pragmatics of purpose.

Yet, as a statement of ideology, I believe that it is desirable for schools to work towards form 3, the integration of processes of enquiry, the deliberate development of metacognition. As I have noted, the evidence that learning transfers from one context to another is limited, but as I have said, that does not, I think, stop one from hoping that schools can organise themselves in order to try to empower their pupils, to deliver what the rhetoric of primary education has so long promised. If reality is to approach the hope, then it is essential, as Bernstein predicted in his work twenty years ago (1975), that a consensus is reached within the school and that staff work together to advance the goals of the integrated approach. It may well be that schools will also be well advised to 'network' with each other.

Now, this implies new ways of working. The education changes of the past decade have done much to break down the notions of teacher autonomy which meant that every class was its own petty commonwealth, and teachers are much more used to planning, deciding and working together. But, as A. Hargreaves (1992) has observed, this often falls short of the full collegiality which is implied by a number of initiatives. Certainly, integration of the sort which I am advocating requires thoroughgoing collaboration, it requires what Rosenholtz (1991) called a 'learning school'. There are, as we well know, many barriers to that. Fullan (1991) and Nias and her colleagues (1992) have shown the degree to which whole-school curriculum development often has small, limited beginnings which may ripple outwards. It is also very dependent on teachers' enthusiasm (and enthusiasms) and, as long as that enthusiasm endures, it is a never-ending activity of enquiry, renewal, revision and extension.

With that in mind, and if the case for a cross-curricular approach has any appeal, it seems sensible to start with the form of integration which is closest to present practice and which, therefore, offers the best chance of success, the best prospect for growth and continuing whole-school curriculum development.

But curriculum development is above all about teacher development, which necessarily leads us to consider how teachers learn, develop and change; and so how they are to be supported, no matter whether they are engaged in complex manoeuvres to integrate the curriculum or in less complex but still tense steps to bring National Curriculum geography or history into their classrooms.

*Chapter 11*

# Professional Development for Primary Humanities

Three areas will be considered, namely initial teacher education (ITE), in-service teacher education (INSET) and the professional learning which may come from the daily experience of teaching and the regular experience of thinking with other professionals. The three categories overlap, so that the experience of teaching affects ITE and INSET, and ITE, in its turn, can shape the way that teaching and INSET are perceived.

This three-fold division needs to be further complicated, since we are interested in professional development for *humanities* teaching. Although I have argued that good educational practices *in general* are related to the ability to do good humanities work, there are things which are special about the humanities, so that it is not enough to be a good all-round teacher (whatever that means) in order to be effective at promoting humanities learning. Stodolsky affirmed that 'instructional arrangements change with the subject taught' (1988, p.xv), which implies that, to a degree, teachers' professional development changes with the subject to be taught.

## Initial teacher education

In England there are two main routes to becoming a teacher. The modern tradition has been for novices to enter higher education (HE) and undertake college-based courses, which include periods of school experience. This pattern hides considerable variations, especially between the first degree plus post-graduate teaching certificate route and the integrated teaching degree route. Academic subject specialist knowledge is more prominent in the former route, while educational and pedagogic subject knowledge are better represented in the second route.

Following Shulman's model of the knowledge which teachers need (see Chapter 3, above), we can see that no one of these three elements (academic, educational and pedagogic) is sufficient, and that all three should be present. However, that leads to overcrowded courses. And still the prospective primary teacher has areas of weakness, knowing, say, a fair amount about human geography, but stinted when it comes to ways of teaching it, and finding himself in difficulties when it comes to RE, which occupied a dark corner of his ITE course. Adler (1984) has argued that in such circumstances novices are thrown back upon their general educational imagination, as a coping strategy. The subject element gets overlaid.

Other questions have been asked about the effectiveness of this form of ITE. Some evidence exists that some people enter ITE with distinct conceptions of teaching which shape what they take note of in the course (Weinstein, 1990; Adler, 1991). This is rather similar to the way in which children's naive concepts interfere with attempts to lead them to better concepts, and is presumably susceptible to similar, time-consuming change strategies (but cf Weinstein, 1990).

An alternative way of inducting people into teaching has revived an older apprenticeship model, where the novice learns mainly on the job, but spends some minor proportion of the working week out of school, perhaps at a university, engaged in guided reflection upon practice and theory. Most of the attractions of this model are obvious, but a less obvious one is that it gets extra adults into the classroom. In the context of this book the crucial problem seems to be that schools have been widely characterised as well-disposed, happy places but with an insufficient sense of academic purpose: good at teaching rather than good at teaching children *something*. We have seen that in the humanities there has been a particular lack of expertise, both in terms of the content and in terms of the methods. Hence it is bizarre to rely on schools to teach novices something in which they are not, themselves, expert. The argument can be extended by noticing that the apprenticeship model puts new teachers in the hands of exactly those people whom governments have consistently excoriated as the source of mediocre educational standards. This can be further developed by asking what these novices are to do: some principled theory of action is necessary in order to shape their experience of being in the classroom in a purposive way. To put it another way, how are these novices to be helped to reflect on education, as opposed to just mimicking someone else's practices?

How might humanities be more prominent in either model of ITE?

It is hard to see how students in England on a four-year degree will get more than 40 hours of contact time devoted to history, with a similar allocation for geography. Those preparing to teach infants may have to make do with half that time.  In the USA there is evidence that students have more cursory encounters with the humanities subjects.  My 1987 English survey of 81 teachers interested in primary history showed that only 37 recalled doing some history teaching method course during their ITE programme, its mean length being estimated at 29 hours.  Yet, given sensible collaboration between the subject associations and tutors in HE institutions, who all face the same problem of helping students to grapple with the same curriculum, it should be possible to share techniques, to pool expertise and to put together series of structured self-study packs, effectively making an informal national curriculum for humanities teacher education.  If such packs were available, then a 40-hour course would be quite adequate to give most student teachers a fair grounding in geography or history.  Granted that the packs could hardly be research-based, they could still prove a useful improvement on the little that exists at the moment.  This may be a pious hope, for collaboration is threatened by the entrepreneurial aggression which is increasingly evident in England's higher education system.

Those who are to be the curriculum co-ordinators of the future  need to cover more content, more techniques, to learn what is implied by the role of curriculum co-ordinator, and to practise some aspect of it.  That time must come out of their subject study time, on the basis that subject study without work on its application is improper preparation for teaching.  Again, it would make sense for interested parties to collaborate in devising national frameworks for this crucial aspect of the teacher's extended role.  One particularly problematic issue which could only benefit from widespread discussion is the topic of this book – the organisation, separation or integration of the primary curriculum.

### In-service education and the humanities

Lip-service is paid to the concept of life-long education, and nowhere more so than in teaching.  In England five days a year are allocated for all teachers to engage in professional activities which do not involve contact with children.  The time was taken from their holiday allowance.  There is also a range of voluntary in-service courses for which fees are charged.  They range from short 'hints for teachers' sessions to award-bearing courses at masters' and doctoral levels.  The 1987 survey of 81 teachers in northwest England found that 40 per cent remembered attending a history INSET course, one-quarter of whom did so at least five years earlier.

As Marbeau (1988) commented regarding the provision of INSET in France to support new ways of doing geography and history, the humanities suffer here, as elsewhere, in the competition for priority with other subjects, especially with the basics. In the interests of institutional development money goes on a plethora of non-subject-specific INSET activities, notably those with 'management' or 'assessment' in the title. As for subject specific-work, the 'basics' dominate.

Teachers want 'practical' INSET, which I understand to mean activities which introduce them to useful techniques and to suitable classroom materials, perhaps putting the two together to show how a particular topic might be taught. Assessing children's performance on the topic has also become a concern, although at the time of writing I cannot commend any published guidance on assessing primary history. Then there is a demand for INSET which helps curriculum co-ordinators by looking at geography or history across the whole school.

Three things seem to be missing from these priorities. One is 'non-practical' INSET. 'Practical' has been hi-jacked, turned into a buzz-word and released as a vacuous slogan. It seems to denote those things which might immediately be used in schools, to be a cover for a modern equivalent of 'tips for teachers'. I quite favour 'tips for teachers', but I insist, too, that there is nothing so practical as a good theory. If the rhetoric of practice has the effect of discouraging reflection on issues such as the scope for integrating the humanities with each other and with other studies; on the absurdities of assessment procedures which have never been informed by the concepts of reliability and validity; or on ways of building into geography activities which demand higher-level thinking of the children, then the curriculum is stultified and teacher professionalism is threatened (which may explain official enthusiasm for 'practical' INSET). In this context it is useful to recall that one powerful approach to teachers' professional development has been to promote the notion of the teacher as a reflective practitioner, someone who is regularly researching into his own practice. What should these reflective practitioners reflect upon? Anything they wish. But, there is a danger here that reflection directed at practice can be deeply limiting, for it is easy to take practices at their face value and to ignore the way in which they have been shaped by societal, institutional and personal factors, which include resources, history (or biography), ideology and routines (Alexander, 1992). Thorough reflection on practice entails drawing upon research evidence and considering these taken-for-granted aspects, and all the more so within a state-mandated curriculum, where it is too easy for teachers to claim that they have no choice but to work as they do.  If reflection and INSET concentrate on practice as a decontexted, common-sense matter of choosing the best methodological hammer to knock in a curriculum nail, then it devalues teaching through never raising the equally important questions about whether glue, screws, dowels or ties would be better ways of fixing, let alone the question of whether the design is the best that is possible in the circumstances anyway.  Through warmly receiving practical INSET teachers can become cultural dupes, agents of their own deprofessionalisation.

The second problem with current INSET provision is that it is implicitly assumed that the teacher needs to know little more about a topic than does the child.  It is easy to see sound pragmatism at work here, especially as children probably will remember little of the content into later life, so that both errors and accuracies are equally likely to be consigned to the oblivion which is the fate of much school learning.  Yet that response misses the point of the discussion in Chapter 3, for without insightful subject matter knowledge the teacher can do little more than string out a series of facts, to be worked on in a dull and passive manner. This is not the aim of the National Curriculum, let alone what people go into teaching to do!

A third thing absent from the prevalent INSET priorities is a sense of long-term planning.  Schools need rolling, medium-term plans so that over five years, say, the school will use INSET to address issues which arise from school development plans, school review and staff appraisal. Planning is necessary, but any attempts to plan are likely to be severely jolted by the repeated diversions in state policy.  Long-term planning, in which there might be a place for the humanities, is regularly sabotaged by moral panics and governmental priorities which have short geneses and short lives too.

So far I have treated INSET as craft-based, short courses.  There are also award-bearing courses at certificate, diploma and master's levels. They allow individuals to go into areas of interest in more detail than do the short, craft courses, and most should involve teachers in reading, reflection, action research and the thoughtful development of practice.

Such courses are threatened.  In England changes in funding policies have meant that schools have come to control their own, meagre INSET budgets, while changing views about INSET have led to the view that it should be school focused (Henderson, 1979).  From that it has been but a small step to say that provision should engage all staff in a primary school on the same issue at the same time, which is entirely consistent with the view of school effectiveness discussed in Chapter 2.  There has also been a feeling that award-bearing INSET programmes are indulgent investigations of recondite philosophies, impracticable practices and radical sociology.

In order to survive, long courses, which award-bearing courses are, have had to become modular (i.e., disjointed), part-time and taught in the evening. Even then, teachers have frequently had to finance themselves, presumably on the assumption that there will be a pay-off in terms of subsequent promotion, for which there is some evidence (Howard and Bradley, 1991).

The resulting fragility of these award-bearing courses implies that teachers' continuing in-service education will be dominated by brief craft sessions which do not involve critical appreciation of the assumptions underpinning practices. In other words, the process of changing teachers from professionals into technicians may be detected at work in INSET.

It is safe to say that humanities INSET has been a fleeting, minority taste. So, where it might be argued that INSET is the natural way in which to advance notions of integration, to further understanding of what geography might achieve, and to encourage thinking about how things might be, the operation of the INSET system means that this is a pipe dream. Only if teachers and schools saw these as priorities would there be much point in considering how these goals might be advanced through INSET. But the evidence is that English teachers do not see problems in the humanities (Wragg *et al*, 1989); nor do Americans in the social studies (Goodlad, 1984, p.184).

In the circumstances it is hard to devise empowering humanities INSET. As with ITE, subject associations and other interested parties could usefully work together on the problem. Unfortunately, the story of the Historical Association's (HA) Diploma for teachers exemplifies the frustrations which dog good intentions. It is open to dispute whether the Diploma was conceived with an eye to the market, and perhaps the validating group might have been otherwise constituted. Perhaps as an awarding body the HA lacked the kudos of a university. Whatever, the programme trickled along for a handful of years and decayed, not for any lack of effort or enthusiasm at the centre, but because of problems of matching provision to the market in circumstances where the humanities market was depressed – as always?

When we consider formal provision of opportunities to learn about primary humanities, whether in ITE or through INSET, the conclusion is simply that opportunities are too few and too brief, and that teachers basically go naked into the classroom. The concept of life-long professional learning may offer a corrective to that dismal assessment.

## Professional development and the humanities

In the past, the patronising assumption was sometimes made that professional development was measured by the number of courses which the teacher had taken. It is now common to see the teacher as the agent of her own development, and courses may – or may not – be an element in that.

Development is perhaps a misnomer, since it is identified with the idea of progress. However, as Huberman (1992) reported in a study of Swiss secondary school teachers, 'development' for a sizeable number of older teachers takes the form of maximising personal satisfaction in life, often by limiting their school commitments. We might also recall Rosenholtz' conclusion that children who were taught by more experienced teachers made less progress with reading (1991).

So, if teachers – especially those in the later stages of their working lives – are to invest time, money, self-esteem and energy in professional development, then that development must prove satisfying. Now, many factors affect whether something is satisfying or not, but two may be remarked upon here. First, if one is forced to do something – to teach about the Tudors, for example – then it is less than likely that one will see the Tudors as an area which is likely to give satisfaction. Of course, views change, and force can concentrate the mind marvellously, as the English government has demonstrated. Power-coercive ways of stimulating professional development include inspection, appraisal, parental comments, the introduction of a mandatory new curriculum, and school review, all of which can be imposed and which can get people to reflect, examine, read and try to be different.

However, endemic ideas, as we saw in Chapter 3, are that satisfaction and choice are associated with each other, and that satisfying activities have pay-offs. Intrinsic motivation, which is when we do something out of interest, not out of compulsion, appears, we saw, to drive many teachers, which is just as well since there are few extrinsic rewards in teaching, let alone in primary humanities. Intrinsic motivation lies at the heart of the notion of the teacher as a life-long learner, someone who is continually renewing herself by her professional actions and thinking about her own practice. Attractive though this view of teacher professionalism is, we need to notice that it is fragile at the best of times, since teachers are so driven by the daily demands of coping with the busy routine of working with so many children (Nias *et al*, 1992). Under these circumstances, Huberman's metaphor of 'tinkering' may be a more accurate description of the extent of this life-long learning, although it still retains the key idea of the teacher as someone who is still interested, on however small a scale, in trying to learn as they work.

A further avenue of professional development is through the teacher, acting as an informed action researcher, becoming engaged in curriculum development, preferably to the benefit of the school as a whole. Much emphasis has been put on this concept, and it has been endorsed in this book. Yet, it will not be the path taken by many teachers, for whom 'tinkering' will represent the limit of their energies, commitment and skills. That is no reason why the idea of the 'extended professional' should not be held up as the ideal, although it must be understood that there are good reasons why many teachers will fall far short of that ideal, many of them lying beyond the teacher's control: 'the preferred *culture* of teaching is just not compatible with the prevailing *context* of teachers' work' (A. Hargreaves, 1992, p.227). As we saw in Chapters 2 and 3, effective work is entwined with the effectiveness of the school, and in schools which are led in ways which encourage learning, risk-taking, collegiality and a sense that professional action can make a difference to children, then whatever the problems of resources, of the area, or which children bring with them to school, there is a force for teachers to learn through their work. That is not to deny Hargreaves' point that where schools are well-supported and where teachers have time to do more than just cope, then learning is more likely to occur. Yet, it can occur anywhere.

But a theme of this book has been that excellence in the individual is not enough, that it needs to be shared with colleagues, to influence and energise them. The quality of a school's leadership is a key variable in whether one person's expertise leads to whole-school curriculum development or not. The school's informal networks are also important, having very different characteristics in 'learning' schools than in 'stuck' ones (Rosenholtz, 1991). By itself, a system of curriculum co-ordinators will not work, since it depends upon the way these two variables work out, not least because it is a Herculean task anyway (Campbell, 1990).

Given the low status of primary humanities, it may therefore be that power-coercive methods will be the most effective in encouraging teachers to develop their skills in this area, although that rather begs the question of how those with power are to be persuaded to coerce those without it. Despite it often being said that extrinsic motivation produces a different response to intrinsic motivation, which is associated with deeper and more committed work, this view is probably over-simplistic. The National Curriculum was imposed, but once colleagues had overcome their initial crossness, many seem to have become genuinely interested in developing ways of working to different standards in curriculum areas with which they were less than familiar. It does not follow that compulsion is necessarily counter-productive, although it does need to be seen as a means to an end, a way of getting others to become interested – in this case interested in the humanities.

Make the assumption that teachers, for whatever reasons, are disposed to be interested, and it follows that serious attempts should be made to present the humanities to teachers in appealing and thoughtful terms. In England both the Geographical Association (GA) and the HA run conferences (and not only in London), they produce low-cost journals directed at primary teachers, and some education authorities, of which Humberside with its admirable *Sources* is one, also produce valuable bulletins (which will disappear soon when English education finances are reformed). I do wonder whether the subject associations have as much influence on the curriculum as do publishers, and I also think that they perpetuate some of the unfortunate characteristics of publishers' practice.

At several points in this book concern has been expressed that school books are deficient, being written to a format to give the market what it wants, with the result that the meretricious has taken precedence over works which start from the question 'what sort of materials *will* promote the key ideas embedded in the National Curriculum?' I am far from convinced that the current crop of National Curriculum materials are good enough, and stories told by colleagues who write such materials suggest that many educational decisions are being made by publishing executives who are bereft of educational insight or whose myopia was developed in the different educational world of some years ago.

Two conclusions can be drawn about teachers' professional development for primary humanities. The first is that the general characteristics of the school matter enormously, so that humanities development is more likely to take place in some sorts of schools than others. Simply making schools *generally* more effective will, I suggest, help the humanities. However, that is not, by itself, sufficient. The second is that there need to be incentives to work in this area and sources of expertise should be readily accessible. Regrettably, even when geography and history are mandatory subjects, this condition is not being adequately met.

## Strategies for advancing professional development in primary humanities

The prospects for primary humanities are uncertain, but trying to improve those prospects depends upon taking a positive stance. A necessary condition for better primary humanities is the existence of 'learning' schools. Nias and her colleagues (1992) saw professional learning taking place through:

● INSET;
● the induction and socialisation of new members of staff;
● teachers working together;
● seeing and hearing others and their work;
● taking responsibility.

Schools and leaders that do not provide opportunities for such activities hardly offer the humanities – or much else – a favourable environment.

To this might be added a list drawn up by Loucks-Horsley (1987, pp.43–4) which contained ten ways in which teacher development could take place outside the INSET/ITE context. Although an appropriate school context is assumed, they are worth repeating here in order to emphasise the range of things which are possible.

● action research;
● curriculum development;
● observing colleague;
● working in teams;
● collaborating through teachers' centres (if there are any left. Perhaps this should be understood as encouragement for different schools to collaborate and network);
● summer schools (especially for getting subject matter knowledge);
● informal networks;
● partnerships (between a school and an ITE institution, for example);
● mentoring beginning teachers;
● an individually guided, expert-advised study programme.

A further four points, largely derived from the discussions above, and which are more focused on the humanities, are:

1. Integration offers one of the most powerful ways of raising the status of primary humanities, particularly that form of integration which portrays the humanities as an area in which powerful metacognitive skills are developed, skills which are important in their own right and which are of value in work on other subjects too. Related to this is the view that the humanities may be an area in which it is *necessary* to develop advanced reading, speaking and writing skills, which cannot be satisfactorily fostered in the splendid isolation of 'English'.

   If integration is conceived in these process terms there is a strong incentive for teachers to see it as an area in which it is important to invest professional energy. It will have to be emphasised that teachers will need not just to understand the processes which unite the humanities but also to appreciate the distinctive concepts, procedures and content of geography and history. The process approach to integration should not become an invitation to revive integration strategies where the vitality of history and geography were submerged under a tedium of reference, copying and comprehension activities.

   Subject associations might usefully consider this line of argument.

2. The humanities may attract attention if emphasis is laid on the degree to which they encourage teacher initiative; allow for topic work; permit local, physically active work; and may be 'child-centred'. In other words, intrinsic interest in the humanities may be stimulated if they are presented as an area in which teachers may wish to take ideologies which they have held and develop them in the context of the curriculum of the 1990s.

3. There is a need for classroom and teacher materials which are based upon the principle of professional development. Prevalent approaches involve favoured teachers broadcasting those aspects of their practice which publishers think will sell: a profoundly conservative approach. Compare it with some of the great curriculum development projects of the 1970s which began by dreaming about what might be and which then wrestled with what was. The up-take may have been disappointing in the short term, but arguably their effects were mis-measured, for the long-term influence of projects such as *Place, Time and Society 8–13*, *Geography for the Young School Leaver*, and *History 13–16* has been considerable.

   Unfashionably, this strategy depends on national materials

production as a key element in professional development. This is perhaps a restatement of the idea that action research – professional learning – should draw upon the insights of others, such as researchers, curriculum theorists, and upon whatever expertise proves relevant to the matter in hand.

4. The matter of ITE/INSET is one of the most intractable, for nothing is more certain than that the ITE programme is already too full and overtaught, and as long as the concept prevails that the new teacher should be in command of all subject areas, it will remain so. I repeat here my suggestion that subject associations should (collaborate to) produce self-study packs which represent a principled view of humanities teaching and learning.

## Chapter 12

# *Lurching after Chimeras?*

Without doubt, the introduction of national curricula to the countries of the UK has helped primary humanities by rescuing them from the practical neglect and parochial curricula of the recent past. No curriculum is beyond criticism and, as we have seen, there have been trenchant criticisms of the English curricula for geography and history, and I have reservations about the Scottish environmental studies scheme. However, they offer a framework and a guaranteed position. They also define the humanities broadly, both in terms of content (although there is, I think, too much emphasis upon the local and national, especially in the Scottish curriculum), and in terms of the procedures which children are to learn. By making this breadth available to children as an entitlement the government has, potentially, empowered them by guaranteeing access to one selection of cultural knowledge and to powerful ways of working.

Whether the same can be said of the reform movements in countries whose humanities curricula are nested within the social studies is another matter, for there is a distinct tension between the prevalent social studies focus on the present and the concern for *then* and *there*. We have also noticed evidence that there can be a tendency to concentrate upon lower-level factual information, and where the UK curricula spell out goals for higher-order learning and require that teachers assess and report children's achievements in relation to those goals, the same does not appear to hold good on an international scale.

Within the UK, then, there is some reason to hope for continuing development in the humanities since a system, albeit an imperfect system, is in place to support them.

But what of the children? The wisdom of the 1980s was that much of the content currently prescribed by UK curricula was inappropriate to them, and there were strong feelings in the 1970s that the humanities had little place in the primary curriculum anyway, being remote and difficult. Evidence has been presented, though, that children can do useful work on place and time. They can interpret and piece together evidence; follow (and later make) maps; use time-lines, construct sequences and work with the number of time; offer explanations, test hypotheses and reason about things, states and peoples; and they can get interested, excited, moved and engaged – both with distant and with immediate affairs.

This extends to infants too, although it is obvious that their abilities are less extensive, less stable and less confidently demonstrated. Yet the recognition of what infants *can* do is a substantial break from an earlier line of research which emphasised what they *could not* do. It also marks a change in teaching methods, for in the past one could simply write off as unsuitable whole areas of human experience. Present practice is characterised by the search for better ways of allowing infants to show what they know and what they misunderstand, as well as by the search for ways of moving them beyond that point. I don't think the aim is to turn out child prodigies so much as to form an awareness in young, impressionable children that there is much more to life than they may have realised from what, despite TV, can be very limited experiences. I also think that it is worth insisting that the humanities can have enormous fascination for young children and that they also constitute admirable vehicles for the development of language, number and expressive powers.

Goodlad, in his substantial study of 'a place called school' (1984) was struck by the way that social studies knowledge was, in the early years of schooling, very human in nature and was strongly related to the children. He was concerned, though, that,

> the topics commonly studied in the [upper elementary] social sciences appear as though they would be of great human interest. But something strange seems to have happened to them on their way to the classroom. The topics of study become removed from their intrinsically human character, reduced to the dates and places readers will recall memorizing for tests (p.212).

There is a warning here, I think, that we can take topics, such as the Tudors and Stuarts, and let the factual clutter overwhelm children's curiosity and get in the way of human understanding. Ironically, the greater our store of one sort of subject matter knowledge (content), the harder it may be to get at that other sort of knowledge which is to do with the key ideas and purposes of the subject: our understanding may become overgrown with the weeds of detail.

One way of helping to humanise the humanities is simply to highlight the human element to the study of other times and other places. This implies a bond between the past and the present, between *here* and *there*. This is not the sort of present-centredness found in many social studies courses, where the past and other places are simply walk-on players, whose part is to provide some point of comparison which shows the wisdom of present arrangements, illustrating that all is for the best in this the best of all possible worlds. Rather, it is an assertion that there is a common humanity about people and that we can – and should – understand others through better understanding ourselves and our lifestyles. Seen in this way the humanities are relevant as a way of understanding people and ourselves better. As I said earlier, it is foolish to exaggerate what children can achieve and the extent to which any grasp they may form of people in geography and history may transform their general understandings. Nevertheless, the humanities is an area of study which may sometimes make a difference to the way children understand others. It is a political and moral decision whether it is worth teaching the humanities for that uncertain, perhaps meagre pay-off. It is a pedagogical question whether it is possible to teach the humanities effectively without having such concerns in mind.

A further way of keeping the humanities human is to take care to deal with children's learning problems. A number have been noted in the course of this book, but perhaps the most significant is that children may have learning problems if they do not know what they are supposed to be learning and why – if their understanding of the name of the game differs from the teacher's. Bennett and Kell (1989) have identified this form of mismatch as a serious problem in teaching four year olds, and there is no reason to believe that it becomes any less serious as children get older. Stress has also been laid on the importance of helping children to appreciate what they have become aware of and learned how to do, and of helping them to apply procedures and concepts learned in one context to problems arising in another. Importance has also been attached to taking the business of concept development seriously, not least by trying to establish the nature of children's misconceptions and then to present learning activities which are designed to modify them.

The issue of subject integration has been a central theme of this book. Some have argued that topic work is inherently more meaningful and relevant to children, a position which I regard with scepticism. However, I have valued integrated approaches of different sorts for different reasons. Some drawing together of history and geography makes great sense, not least in terms of time management, where they share the same content, always given that the teacher is clear exactly which history and geography have priority. Local studies are the obvious case where the subjects could purposefully merge. Integration of the humanities with other subjects also makes practical sense, so that scientific ideas to do with floating and sinking are developed (perhaps not entirely happily) in conjunction with work on the topic 'ships and seafarers'. I have suggested that it might help the status of the humanities if a good part of the English curriculum were seen to be confronted and assessed through work on time and place. There will also be times when it makes sense to do a straight geography or history topic – on volcanoes, for example – and there will be plenty of occasions when a history or geography theme dominates a topic, with the attendant subjects very much taking on a well-defined, subordinate role. That said, I see little by way of a case for demarcated, consistent single subject teaching.

One reason for emphasising the scope for curriculum integration is that the introduction of national curricula provides the opportunity to analyse the processes of enquiry and of representation which are common to a clutch of subjects and to pull the school curriculum together through deliberately developing conscious enquiry habits which have common characteristics in a range of subjects. Indeed, there will be techniques which are special to *this* subject or to *that*, but what they have in common is greater, I believe, than what separates them. This is a belief, and I have observed that the evidence that learning in one domain can be transferred to others is equivocal. But the prospect it holds out of inducting children into more powerful ways of learning, of empowering them, is sufficiently attractive to make me believe that it is worth pursuing. It can only be done on a whole-school basis, for nothing is plainer than that this is not something which will show fruit at the end of one year in an enthusiast's class.

Is this vision of a more human, powerful, vibrant humanities a chimera, a fantastic dream? Rosenholtz said that teachers' power to dream is important, so perhaps it may not matter if it is a chimera. But can we pursue it, or are the conditions under which teachers now work such that the best that can be managed is a lurch towards it?

One condition which severely limits many teachers' ability to join the quest (should they wish to do so), is their lack of subject matter understanding. Just as it is important for children to understand the procedures and ideas behind their humanities topic, so too teachers need to know not just the content, but also to understand the deep structure of the subject, its purposes and nature, and to have a repertoire of activities that are powerful at helping children to see beyond the detail of Tudor witchcraft and Third World privation. ITE and INSET are obvious sources of this sort of knowledge, while classroom materials are equally important, if less obvious. Unfortunately, I have questioned the potency of ITE/INSET in this area, and wondered about the slick new materials being published for classroom use.

Much will fall upon the semi-specialist, the curriculum co-ordinator. Whether that system can ever deliver what is hoped of it must be an open question. It is unlikely that alternatives would be better. It has been argued that there is a case for most of the humanities teaching in a school being done by the co-ordinator, with other semi-specialists doing the music or science work in her class. The tradition of the generalist class teacher, to which many colleagues are attached, militates against this, although, as Alexander (1984; 1992) explained, the case for the generalist has not been proven. Whatever the co-ordinator's role, it is possible that the system would work a lot better if much more serious thought were given – by the subject associations in particular – to what the curriculum co-ordinator, who we can assume is a skilled all-round educationist, needs to know about learning and teaching the humanities. And it goes without saying that the system will work better where school management supports co-ordinators (which is by no means the normal state of affairs), and that it works best where the school has the characteristics of an effective school, as discussed in Chapter 2.

This too is a recurrent theme, that good humanities practice needs good schools. Pockets of goodness can exist in individual classrooms anywhere, but since our concern is with the total educational experience of children from aged 5 to 11, we are not interested in pockets, but in whole-school quality. Changes in the English education system may encourage schools to become even better than they already are, but they may impede developments in lower status curriculum areas, such as the humanities. For example, putting schools into competition with each other, using raw-score league tables of results dominated by children's scores in the core subjects, may encourage schools to concentrate on these subjects to the detriment of the others. Again, a new system of school inspection will replace the local authority advisers who sometimes were great sources of guidance on the development of good humanities work. In the case of a well-developed, well-resourced priority subject such as mathematics, that may not matter, but it could prove serious for the foundling, marginal subjects.

So, we return to the idea of lurching. Is the condition of the educational system such that teachers are scarcely able to do much more than to stagger towards ideals, particularly if those ideals amount to going beyond (or counter to) the national curricula in any way? In other words, has teacher professionalism been limited to argument about how to improve children's scores on purblind reading tests?

You are better placed than I to answer that. In the hope that many teachers still feel that they have the energy and that they can create the room to take the curriculum and shake it into a shape which is educationally productive and comfortable for them, their pupils and their colleagues, I want to end with two sets of ideas. The first deals with a comment made by one reader of a draft version of this book: 'but what do we do?'. The second is a list of things which it would be helpful to know more about. It may suggest ideas for practitioner research and encourage additions to our store of evidence about primary humanities.

What might schools wishing to take control of *their* curriculum, as a whole, do?

- Start with the humanities. The advantages are that these are not high-status subjects where a lot rides on getting it right, first time. Moreover, as marginal subjects, people have less face to lose by experimenting and not succeeding. Lastly, the National Curriculum has reconceptualised the nature of good humanities practice, so that what was yesterday's dogma is often discredited today, with the result that we all start on a nearly level playing field.
- Work out from methods with which people feel happy. It might be better to improve the quality of recitation lessons as a start, rather than begin by trying to transform established ways of working – that can come later.
- Aim for teaching guide-lines – for example the four Ss – Select, Sloganise, Structure, Spread (the general processes and ideas from humanities to other subjects).
- Local geography and history topics offer a good chance of success. If possible, involve the English co-ordinator.
- Go for simple integrations first, then capitalise on success in order to move on to more complex forms.
- Try taking a topic like 'Our place' and run it through as a whole-school topic (Key Stage 1 and Key Stage 2) for a term. Have older children work with younger, and take every opportunity to get colleagues working with and learning from each other.

● Read a good book on teaching geography (Weigand, 1992) or history (Cooper, 1992). When it comes to classroom materials, class sets of one text are less good than fewer copies each of a range of books.
● If your school takes student teachers on school experience, ask that you be given a group of humanities specialists with a brief to undertake a development project.
● Continue to try to find room to learn by engaging in action research, informed by the findings of others looking at similar problems.

Some issues concerning primary humanities which need further study include:

● what is the relationship between gender and performance?
● what interests children – or is interest something generated by the teacher?
● the nature of cognitive development in the context of primary humanities, both in its own right and with reference to other curriculum subjects – or to put it another way, how accurate is the developmental map contained in the National Curriculum?
● the development of humanities concepts and misconceptions;
● evidence of effective approaches to teaching different topics within the humanities;
● ways of teaching 'higher order' humanities skills and concepts;
● language and the humanities;
● the characteristics of more – and less – effective humanities classroom materials;
● group-work;
● whether general, transferable skills and metacognition can be developed through the humanities – and if so, to what extent and how?
● methods of assessment, including how to translate attainment target statements into fair tests, and how to grade and moderate children's responses;
● how to help children to be intelligent, independent learners, as presaged by the history document;
● methods for encouraging children to relate the past and the present, here and there, in a way which fosters an awareness of the common humanity behind diversity;
● the nature of effective ITE for general classroom teachers and for

- potential curriculum co-ordinators;
- likewise, but with reference to INSET;
- factors encouraging and discouraging professional and curriculum development in the humanities.

Curriculum targets and content may be prescribed to a greater or lesser extent but it is still up to teachers to implement those prescriptions, which guarantees that the curriculum that is taught is different from the one which the government planned. Moreover, the government has essentially left the choice of teaching methods to teachers, and since pedagogy is arguably as central an element of the curriculum as is content, this too gives teachers enormous scope for the exercise of professional judgement. To a much greater extent than is often recognised the primary curriculum is in the hands of primary teachers, particularly in an area such as this where there is little, existing research knowledge which could be used to inform our thinking.

However, under pressure and over-worked, they may not feel that this is a liberty which they can exploit. But it is a liberty which, in a calmer future, extended professionals with lively, enquiring minds will be able to turn to good advantage. Teacher autonomy may have been curbed by the National Curriculum but it has not been killed. The humanities, relatively uncharted territory, are a splendid area in which to demonstrate that.

# References

Adey, P., Shayer, M. and Yates, C. (1990) *Better Learning* (London: King's College).

Adler, S. (1984) 'A field study of selected student teacher perspectives towards social studies', *Theory and Research in Social Education*, 12(1), 13–30.

Adler, S. A. (1991) 'The education of social studies teachers', in J. P. Shaver, *op cit*.

Alexander, R. (1984) *Primary Teaching* (London: Cassell).

Alexander, R. (1992) *Policy and Practice in Primary Education* (London: Routledge).

Alexander, R., Rose, J. and Woodhead, C. (1992) *Curriculum Organisation and Classroom Practice in Primary Schools: a discussion paper* (London: DES).

Alleman, J. E. and Rosaen, C. L. (1991) 'The cognitive, social-emotional and moral development characteristics of students', in J. P. Shaver, *op cit*.

Anderson, L. W. and Burns, R. B. (1989) *Research in Classrooms* (Oxford: Pergamon Press).

Anderson, L. W., Ryan, D. W. and Shapiro, B. J. (eds) (1989) *The IEA Classroom Environment Study* (Oxford: Pergamon).

Apple, M. (1986) *Teachers and Texts* (London: Routledge).

Argyris, C., Putnam, R. and Smith, D. (1985) *Action Science* (San Francisco: Jossey Bass).

Atkinson, R. F. (1978) *Knowledge and Explanation in History* (London: Macmillan).

Bale, J. (1987) *Geography in the Primary School* (London: Routledge).

Barnes, R. (1989) *Art, Design and Topic Work 8–13* (London: Allen and Unwin).

Bartz, B. S. (1970) 'Maps in the classroom', *Journal of Geography* 69.

Beck, I. L., McKeown, M. G. and Gromall, E. W. (1989) 'Learning from social studies texts', *Cognition and Instruction*, 6(2), 99–158.

Bell, C. H. (1991) *Developing a European Dimension in Primary Schools* (London: David Fulton).

Bennett, N. (1988) 'The effective primary school teacher', *Teaching and Teacher Education*, 4(1), 19–30.

Bennett, N. and Kell, J. (1989) *A Good Start? Four Year Olds in Infant Schools* (Oxford: Blackwell).

Bennett, N., Desforges, C. W., Cockburn, A. and Wilkinson, B. (1984) *The Quality of Pupil Learning Experience* (London: LEA).

Bennett, R. J. (1989) 'Whither models and geography in a post welfarist state?', in B. MacMillan, *op cit.*

Bernstein, B. (1975) *Class, Codes and Control, Vol 3*, (London: Routledge).

Blades, M. and Spencer, C. (1986) 'Map use by young children', *Geography*, 71(1), 47–53.

Blaut, J. M. and Stea, D. (1971) 'Studies in geographic learning', *Annals of the Association of American Geographers*, 61, 387–393.

Bloch, M. (1954) *The Historian's Craft* (Manchester: Manchester University Press).

Blyth, A. *et al* (1976) *Place, Time and Society 8–13: curriculum planning in history, geography and social science* (Bristol: ESL/Collins).

Blyth, J. E. (1977) 'Young children and the past' (Southampton: unpublished MEd. dissertation).

Boardman, D. (1989) 'The development of graphicacy: children's understanding of maps', *Geography*, 74(4), 321–31.

Booth, M. (1979) 'A longitudinal study of cognitive skills, concepts and attitudes', (Reading: unpublished PhD. thesis).

Bradbeer, J. (1991) 'The greening of geography', *The New Academic*, 1(1), 13–14.

Bradley Commission (1988) *Building a History Curriculum* (Washington DC: Educational Excellence Network).

Brophy, J. (1990a) 'Teaching social studies for understanding', *Elementary School Journal*, 90(4), 351–417.

Brophy, J. (1990b) *Mary Lake: a case study of fifth grade social studies (American history)* (East Lansing, Michigan: Michigan State University).

Brophy, J. (ed.) (1991) *Advances in Research on Teaching, Vol 2* (Greenwich, Connecticut: JAI Press Inc.).

Brophy, J. (1992) 'The *de facto* national curriculum in U.S. elementary social studies: a critique of a representative sample', *Journal of*

*Curriculum Studies*, 24(5), 401–48.

Brophy, J. E and Good, T. L. (1986) 'Teacher behavior and student achievement', in M. Wittrock, *op cit.*

Brophy, J., McMahon, S. and Prawat, R. (1991) 'Elementary social studies series: critique of a representative example by six experts', *Social Education*, 55(3), 155–60.

Brown, A. L. and DeLoache, J. S. (1983) 'Metacognitive skills', in M. Donaldson (ed.) *Early Childhood Development and Education* (Oxford: Blackwell).

Burroughs, S. G. (1988) 'Topic based curricular approaches in the primary school', *Early Child Development and Care*, 37, 141–62.

Campbell, J. (1990) 'Curriculum co-ordinators, the National Curriculum and the aims of primary education', in N. Proctor (ed.) *The Aims of Primary Education* (Lewes: The Falmer Press).

Camperell, K. and Knight, R. S. (1991) 'Reading research and social studies', in J. P. Shaver, *op cit.*

Cangelosi, J. S. (1991) *Evaluating Classroom Instruction* (New York: Longman).

Case, R. (1985) *Intellectual Development* (London: Academic Press).

Catling, S. (1990a) 'Subjecting geography to the national curriculum', *The Curriculum Journal*, 1(1), 77–90.

Catling, S. (1990b) 'Early mapwork: mapwork with 5 to 8 year olds', in *Primary Geography Matters* (Sheffield: The Geographical Association).

Chappell, J. E. (1989) 'Relations between geography and other disciplines', in M. S. Kenzer (ed.) *On Becoming a Professional Geographer* (Columbus, Ohio: Merrill).

Checkland, P. (1981) *Systems Thinking, Systems Practice* (London: John Wiley).

Clark, C. and Peterson, P. L. (1986) 'Teachers' thought processes', in M. Wittrock, *op cit.*

Clark, K. (1992) 'Speech to the North of England Conference', 3.1.92 (Southport).

Clarke, G., Sears, A. and Smyth, J. (1990) *A Proposal to Revise the Elementary Social Studies Curriculum* (Fredericton, NB: University of New Brunswick).

Collingwood, J. (1946) *The Idea of History* (Oxford: Oxford University Press).

Collingwood, J. (1959) 'History as re-enactment of past experience', in P. Gardiner, *op cit.*

Coltham, J. B. (1960) 'Junior school children's understanding of some terms', (Manchester: unpublished PhD. thesis).

Cooper, H. (1992) *The Teaching of History* (London: David Fulton).

Cosgrove, D. (1989) 'Models, description and imagination in geography', in B. Macmillan, *op cit.*

Craft, A. (1991) 'Thinking skills and the whole curriculum', *The Curriculum Journal*, 2(2), 183-99.

Craft, A. (1992) 'Cross-curricular work', *Journal of Teacher Development*, 1(2), 77–89.

Cuban, L. (1991) 'History of teaching in social studies', in J. P. Shaver, *op cit.*

Curtis, C. K. (1991) 'Social studies for students at risk and with disabilities', in J. P. Shaver, *op cit.*

David, T., Curtis, A. and Siraj-Blatchford, I. (1992) *Effective Learning in the Early Years* (Warwick: University of Warwick).

Department of Education and Science (1978) *Primary Education in England: a survey by HM Inspectors of Schools* (London: HMSO).

Department of Education and Science (1989a) *The Teaching and Learning of History and Geography* (London: HMSO).

Department of Education and Science (1989b) *English in the National Curriculum* (London: HMSO).

Department of Education and Science (1990a) *The Teaching and Learning of Reading in Primary Schools* (London: DES).

Department of Education and Science (1990b) *Aspects of Education in New York* (London: HMSO).

Department of Education and Science (1991a) *Statement by the Secretary of State for Education and Science*, 3.12.91.

Department of Education and Science (1991b) *Geography 5–16* (London: HMSO).

Department of Education and Science (1991c) *History 5–16* (London: HMSO).

Department of Education and Science (1991d) *Aspects of Primary Education in France* (London: DES).

Desforges, C. W. and Cockburn, A. (1987) *Understanding the Mathematics Teacher* (Lewes: The Falmer Press).

Desforges, C. W. and McNamara, D. (1978) 'One man's heuristic is another man's blindfold', *British Journal of Teacher Education*, 3(1), 27–40.

Dickinson, A. (1990) 'Assessment', in R. Aldrich (ed.) *History in the National Curriculum* (London: Kogan Page).

Dillon, J. T. (1982) 'The effects of questions in education and other enterprises', *Journal of Curriculum Studies*, 14(2), 127–52.

Dillon, J. T. (1988) *Questioning and Teaching. A Manual of Practice* (London: Croom Helm).

Donaldson, M. (1978) *Children's Minds* (London: Croom Helm).

Dowling, P. and Noss, R. (eds) (1990) *Mathematics versus the National Curriculum* (Lewes: The Falmer Press).

Downey, M. and Levstik, L. (1991) 'Teaching and learning history', in J. P. Shaver, *op cit.*

Doyle, W. (1983) 'Academic work', *Review of Educational Research,* 53(2), 159–99.

Doyle, W. (1986) 'Classroom organization and management', in M. Wittrock, *op cit.*

Doyle, W. and Ponder, G. A. (1977/8), 'The practicality ethic in teacher decision-making', *Interchange,* 8(3),1–12.

Dufour, B. (ed.) (1990) *The New Social Curriculum* (Cambridge: Cambridge University Press).

Egan, K. (1979) *Educational Development,* (New York: Oxford University Press).

Elliott, J. (1991a) *Action Research for Educational Change* (Milton Keynes: Open University Press).

Elliott, J. (1991b) 'Teachers in action', *Primary Associations,* 1(1), 21–4.

Entrikin, J. N. (1989) '*The Nature of Geography* in perspective', in J. N. Entrikin and S. D. Brunn (eds) *Reflections on Richard Hartshorne's 'The Nature of Geography'* (Washington: Association of American Geographers).

Evans, R. W. (1989) 'Diane Ravitch and the revival of history: a critique', *The Social Studies,* 80, 85–91.

Ferrario, M. (1991) 'Sex differences in leadership style: myth or reality?', *Women in Management Review and Abstracts* 6(3), 16–21.

Fines, J. (1982) 'Looking at history', in J. Nixon (ed.) *Drama and the Whole Curriculum* (London: Hutchinson).

Fines, J. (1992) 'Stocktaking', *Times Educational Supplement,* 17.4.92, 39.

Fisher, S. and Hicks, D. (1985) *World Studies 8–13: A teachers' handbook* (Edinburgh: Oliver and Boyd).

Flavell, J. H. (1985) *Cognitive Development,* second edition, (Engelwood Cliffs, NJ: Prentice Hall).

Fullan, M. (1991) *The New Meaning of Educational Change* (London: Cassell).

Galton, M. (1989) *Teaching in the Primary School* (London: David Fulton).

Galton, M. and Patrick, H. (1990) *Curriculum Provision in the Small Primary School* (London: Routledge).

Galton, M. and Williamson, J. (1992) *Group-work in the Primary Classroom* (London: Routledge).

Gardiner, P. (1959) *The Nature of Historical Explanation* (Oxford: Oxford University Press).

Gayford, C. (1991) 'Environmental education: a question of emphasis in the school curriculum', *Cambridge Journal of Education*, 21(1), 73–9.

Ghaye, A. L. and Robinson, E. G. (1987) 'Concept maps and children's thinking: a constructivist approach', in F. Slater (ed.) *Language Learning in the Teaching of Geography* (London: Routledge).

Goodlad, J. (1984) *A Place Called School: prospects for the future* (New York: McGraw-Hill).

Goodson, I. (1983) *School Subjects and Curriculum Change* (London: Croom Helm).

Goodson, I. (1988) *The Making of Curriculum* (Lewes: The Falmer Press).

Gordon, P. (1991) *Teaching the Humanities* (London: The Woburn Press).

Graves, N. J. (1975) *Geography in Education* (London: Heinemann).

Graves, N. J., Kent, A., Lambert, D., Naish, M. and Slater, F. (1990) 'Evaluating the final report', *Teaching Geography* 15(4), 147–51.

Gritzner, C. F. (1982) 'What is right with geography', *Journal of Geography* 81(6), 237–9.

Haas, M. (1988) *An Analysis of the Geographic Concepts and Locations in Elementary Social Studies Textbooks* (Morgantown: West Virginia University).

Haas, M. (1989) *Teaching Geography in the Elementary School* (Bloomington In: ERIC clearing house for social studies).

Hahn, C. (1991) *'Controversial issues in social studies'* in J. P. Shaver, *op cit.*

Hallam, R. N. (1975) 'A study of the effect of teaching method on the growth of logical thought with specific reference to history' (Leeds: unpublished PhD. thesis).

Hargreaves, A. (1992) 'Cultures of teaching: a focus for change', in A. Hargreaves and M. Fullan (eds) *Understanding Teacher Development* (London: Cassell).

Hargreaves, D. (1984) 'Teacher questions: open, closed and half-open', *Educational Research*, 26(1), 46-51.

Hargreaves, D. (1991) 'Coherence and manageability: reflections on the national curriculum and cross-curricular provision', *Curriculum Journal*, 2(1), 33–41.

Harlen, W. and Osborne, R. (1985) 'A model for learning and teaching applied to primary science', *Journal of Curriculum Studies*, 17(2), 133–46.

Harling, P. (1990) *100s of Ideas for Primary Maths* (London: Hodder and Stoughton).

Harvey, D. (1989) 'From models to Marx', in B. Macmillan, *op cit.*

Hawkins, G. (1990/1) 'CG7; points of view', *Streetwise*, 5, 5.

Henderson E. S. (1979) 'The concept of school-focused education and training', *British Journal of Teacher Education*, 5(1).

Her Majesty's Inspectors of Schools (1985) *History in the Primary and Secondary Years* (London: HMSO).

Her Majesty's Inspectors of Schools (1990) Standards in Education, (London: DES).

Her Majesty's Inspectors of Schools (1991) *Inspection of Humanities Courses in Years 5–9 in 26 Schools* (London: DES).

Hicks, D. (1981) 'Teaching about other peoples: how biased are school books?', *Education 3–13*, 9(2), 14–18.

Hicks, D. and Steiner, M. (eds) (1989) *Making Global Connections: a world studies workbook* (Edinburgh: Oliver and Boyd).

Hirst, P. (1965) 'Liberal education and the nature of knowledge', in R. D. Archambault (ed.) *Philosophical Analyses and Education* (London: Routledge).

Howard, J. and Bradley, H. (1991) *Patterns of Employment and Development of Teachers after INSET Courses* (Cambridge: Cambridge Institute of Education).

Howson, G. (1991) *National Curricula in Mathematics* (Leicester: The Mathematical Association).

Huberman, M. (1992) 'Teacher development and instructional mastery', in A. Hargreaves and M. Fullan (eds) *Understanding Teacher Development* (London: Cassell).

Huckle, J. (1990) 'Environmental education: teaching for a sustainable future', in B. Dufour, *op cit.*

Jencks, C. *et al* (1972) *Inequality* (London: Allen Lane).

Johnston, K. (1988) 'Changing teachers' conceptions of teaching and learning', in J. Calderhead (ed.) *Teachers' Professional Learning*, (Lewes: The Falmer Press).

Johnston, R. J. (1991) *Geography and Geographers: Anglo-American geography since 1945*, 4th edition (London: Edward Arnold).

Joyce, W. W., Little, T. H. and Wronski, S. P. (1991) 'Scope and sequence, goals and objectives: effects on social studies', in J. P. Shaver, *op cit.*

Kleibard, H. M. (1986)*The Struggle for the American Curriculum* (New York: Routledge).

Knight, P. T. (1988) 'Children's understanding of people in the past' (Lancaster: unpublished PhD. thesis).

Knight, P. T. (1989a) 'Children's concepts, the curriculum and change', *Curriculum,* 10(1), 5–12.

Knight, P. T. (1989b) 'Empathy: concept, confusion and consequences in a national curriculum', *Oxford Review of Education,* 15(1), 41–54.

Knight, P. T. (1989c) 'A study of teaching and children's understanding of people in the past', *Research in Education,* 44, 39–53.

Knight, P. T. (1991a) 'Teaching as exposure: the case of history in key stage 2', *British Education Research Journal,* 17(2), 129–40.

Knight, P. T. (1991b) *History at Key Stages 1 and 2* (London: Longman).

Knight, P. T. (1992) 'Myth and legend at Key Stage One – the case of Robin Hood', *Primary Teaching Studies,* 7(1), 237–44.

Kruger, C., Summers, M. and Palacio, D. (1990) 'Adding forces – a target for primary science INSET', *British Journal of In-service Education,* 16(1) 4 –52.

Kurfman, D. G. (1991) 'Testing as context for social education', in J. P. Shaver, *op cit.*

Kyriacou, C. (1991) *Essential Teaching Skills* (Oxford: Blackwell).

Lee, P. J. (1983) 'History teaching and philosophy of history', *History and Theory, Beiheft 22,* 19–49.

Leming, J. S. (1991) 'Teacher characteristics and social studies education', in J. P. Shaver, *op cit.*

Levstik, L. and Yessin, R. (1990) 'I prefer success' (paper presented to AERA: Boston Ma.).

Lewis, D. (1987) 'Writing in a humanities classroom', in F. Slater (ed.) (1987) *Language Learning in the Teaching of Geography* (London: Routledge).

Long, S. (1987) 'Supporting teachers and children in topic work', in S. Tann, *op cit.*

Loucks-Horsley, S. (1987) *Continuing to Learn: a guidebook for teacher development* (Andover Ma.: Regional Laboratory for Educational Development).

Low-Beer, A. (1986) 'The eclipse of history in New Zealand schools', *New Zealand Journal of Educational Studies* (1992), 113–22.

Lyle, S. (1989) 'Forest environments', in D. Hicks and M. Steiner (eds)

*Making Global Connections: a world studies workbook* (Edinburgh: Oliver and Boyd).

Macmillan, B. (ed.) (1989) *Remodelling Geography* (Oxford: Blackwell).

Manson, G. (1981) 'Notes on the status of geography in American schools', *Journal of Geography* 80(6), 244–48.

Marbeau, L. (1988) 'History and geography in elementary school', *Western European Education* 20(2), 14–43.

Marsden, W. (1988) 'Continuity and change in geography textbooks: perspectives from the 1930s to the 1960s', *Geography,* 73(4), 327–40.

Marsden, W. (1991) 'Non-local locality studies', *Primary Geography,* 7(2).

Marsh, C. J. (1987) 'Implementation of a social studies curriculum in an Australian elementary school', *Elementary School Journal,* 87(4), 475–86.

Martin, R. (1977) *Historical Explanation: re-enactment and practical inference* (Ithaca: Cornell University Press).

Martorella, P. (1991) 'Knowledge and concept development in social studies', in J. P. Shaver, *op cit.*

Marwick, A. (1970) *The Nature of History* (London: Macmillan).

Matthews, M. H. (1984) 'Cognitive mapping abilities of young boys and girls', *Geography,* 69(4), 327–36.

McCulloch, G. (1992) *The School Curriculum in New Zealand: history, theory, policy and practice* (Palmerston North: the Dunmore Press).

McNamara, D. (1980) 'The outsider's arrogance: the failure of participant observers to understand classroom events', *British Educational Research Journal* 6(20), 113–27.

McNamara, D. and Pettitt, D. (1991) 'Can research inform classroom practice?', *Teaching and Teacher Education,* 7(4), 395–403.

Meck, R. (1986) 'Native North Americans: a project approach to counter stereotyping', *Primary Teaching Studies,* 2(1), 37–42.

Mehlinger, H. D. (1991) 'The National Commission on Social Studies in Schools: an example of the politics of curriculum reform in the U.S.A.', *Journal of Curriculum Studies,* 23(5), 449–65.

Milburn, D. (1972) 'Children's vocabulary', in N. Graves (ed.) *New Movements in the Study and Teaching of Geography* (London: Temple Smith).

Milner, D. (1983) *Children and Race Ten Years On* (London: Ward Lock).

Mink, L. O. (1973) 'The divergence of history and sociology in the recent philosophy of history', in B. Suppes *et al* (eds) *Logic,*

*Methodology and Philosophy of Science IV* (Amsterdam: North Holland Publishing Company).

Molyneux, F. and Tolley, H. (1987) *Teaching Geography: a teaching skills workbook* (London: Macmillan).

Morgan, W. (1992) *Geography in the National Curriculum: planning for Key Stage 2* (Sheffield: The Geographical Association).

Morris, J. M. (1992) 'Back to the future: the impact of political ideology on the design and implementation of the national curriculum', *Curriculum Journal,* 3(1), 75–85.

Mortimore, P., Sammons, P., Stoll, L., Lewis, D. and Ecob, R. (1988) *School Matters* (Wells: Open Books).

Muessig, R. H. (1987) 'An analysis of developments in geographic education', *Elementary School Journal,* 87(5), 519–30.

Murphy, J. (1990) 'A most respectable prejudice; inequality in educational research and policy', *British Journal of Sociology,* 41(1), 29–54.

National Association for Environmental Education (1992) *Environmental Education* (Walsall: NAEE).

National Curriculum Council (1990a) *Curriculum Guidance 7: Environmental Education* (York: NCC).

National Curriculum Council (1990b) *Curriculum Guidance 8: Education for Citizenship* (York: NCC).

National Writing Project (1989) *Becoming a Writer* (Walton-on-Thames: Nelson).

Nias, J., Southworth, G. and Campbell, P. (1992) *Whole School Curriculum Development in the Primary School* (Lewes: The Falmer Press).

Nickell, P. (1992) 'Doing the stuff of social studies', *Social Education,* 56(2), 91–4.

Noble, P. (1991) *Primary History Today* (London: The Historical Association).

Oakeshott, M. (1983) *On History and Other Essays* (Oxford: Blackwell).

Oakland, J. S. (1989) *Total Quality Management* (Oxford: Butterworth-Heinemann).

Olson, J. (1980) 'Teacher constraints and curriculum change', *Journal of Curriculum Studies,* 12(1), 1–11.

O'Reilly, D. (1990) 'Hierarchies in mathematics', in P. Dowling and R. Noss, op cit.

Orton, J. D. and Weick, K. E. (1990) 'Loosely coupled systems: a reconceptualisation', *Academy of Management Review,* 15(2),

203–223.

Osborn, M. and Broadfoot, P. (1992) 'A lesson in progress? Primary classrooms observed in England and France', *Oxford Review of Education*, 18(1), 3–15.

Osborne, R. and Freyberg, P. (1985) *Learning in Science* (London: Heinemann).

Parker, W. C. (1991) 'Achieving thinking and decision-making objectives in social studies', in J. P. Shaver, *op cit.*

Parsons, C. (1986) *The Curriculum Change Game* (Lewes: The Falmer Press).

Perret-Clermont, A. (1980) *Social Interaction and Cognitive Development in Children* (London: Academic Press).

Peters, T. J. and Waterman, R. H. (1982) *In Search of Excellence: lessons from America's best-run companies* (New York: Harper and Row).

Peterson, P. L. (1979) 'Direct instruction reconsidered', in P. L. Peterson and H. J. Wahlberg (eds) *Research on Teaching* (Berkeley, Ca: McCutcheon).

Phenix, P. H. (1964) *Realms of Meaning* (New York: McGraw-Hill).

Piaget, J. (1981) *Intelligence and Affectivity* (Berkeley Ca: Annual Reviews Inc.).

Pigozzi, B. W. (1990) *A View on Geography and Elementary Education* (East Lansing MN: Institute for Research on Teaching).

Pike, G. and Selby, D. (1988) *Global Teacher, Global Learner* (Sevenoaks: Hodder and Stoughton).

Pollard, A. and Tann, S. (1987) *Reflective Teaching in the Primary School* (London: Cassell).

Popkewitz, T. S. (ed.) (1987) *The Formation of School Subjects: the struggle for creating an American institution* (Lewes: The Falmer Press).

Porter, A. (1991) 'Controversial issues in the humanities: helping pupils to handle bias', in P. Gordon, *op cit.*

Preston, M. (1987) *Mathematics in Primary Education* (Lewes: The Falmer Press).

Pring, R. (1976) *Knowledge and Schooling* (London: Open Books).

Purkey, S. and Smith, M. S. (1983) 'Effective schools: a review', *Elementary School Journal*, 83(4), 427–52.

Ramsden, P. (1993) 'What is good teaching in higher education?', In P. T. Knight (ed.) *The Audit and Assessment of Teaching Quality* (Birmingham: SCED).

Relph, E. (1976) *Place and Placelessness* (London: Pion Limited).

Rhys, W. (1972) 'The development of logical thinking', in N. Graves (ed.) *New Movements in the Study and Teaching of Geography* (London: Temple Smith).

Rogers, C. (1990) 'Motivation in the primary years', in C. Rogers and P. Kutnick (eds) *The Social Psychology of the Primary School* (London: Routledge).

Rosenholtz, S. J. (1991) *Teachers' Workplace* (New York: Longman).

Rosenshine, B. (1983) 'Teaching functions in instructional programs', *Elementary School Journal,* 83(4), 335–51.

Royal Geographical Society (1950/76) 'Geography and social studies in schools', in M. Williams (ed.) *Geography and the Integrated Curriculum: a reader* (London: Heinemann).

Sammons, P. and Mortimore, P. (1990) 'Pupil achievement and pupil alienation in the junior school', in J. Docking (ed.) *Education and Alienation in the Junior School* (Lewes: The Falmer Press).

Schon, D. (1987) *Educating the Reflective Practitioner* (New York: Basic Books).

Scottish Office Education Department (1992) *Working Paper No. 13: Environmental Studies 5–14* (Edinburgh: The Scottish Office).

Selby, D. (1991) 'Towards an irreducible global perspective in school', *Westminster Studies in Education,* 14, 27–35.

Shaver, J. P. (1987) 'What should be taught in social studies?', in V. Richardson-Koehler (ed.) *Educator's Handbook: a research perspective* (New York: Longman).

Shaver, J. P. (1991) *Handbook of Research on Social Studies Teaching and Learning* (New York: Macmillan).

Shemilt, D. (1980) *History 13–16 Evaluation Study* (Edinburgh: Holmes McDougall).

Shennan, M. (1991) *Teaching About Europe* (London: Cassell).

Shuell, T. J. (1992) 'Designing instructional computing systems for meaningful learning', in P. Winne and M. Jones (eds) *Foundations and Frontiers in Instructional Computing Systems* (New York: Springer Verlag).

Shulman, L. (1986) 'Those who understand: knowledge growth in teaching', *Educational Researcher,* 15, 4–14.

Shulman, L. (1987) 'Knowledge and teaching foundations of the new reform', *Harvard Education Review,* 57(1), 1–22.

Simon, J. (1992) 'Social studies: the cultivation of social amnesia?', in G. McCulloch, *op cit.*

Slater, F. (1992) ' ... to travel with a different view', in M. Naish (ed.) *Geography and Education* (London: Institute of Education).

Slavin, R. E. (1990) *Cooperative Learning: theory, research and practice* (Needham Heights, Ma: Allyn and Bacon).

Smith, D. J. and Tomlinson, S. (1989) *The School Effect* (London: The Policy Studies Institute).

Smith, L. (1986) 'From psychology to instruction', in J. Harris (ed.) *Child Psychology in Action* (London: Croom Helm).

Smith, L. and Knight, P. T. (1992) 'Adolescent reasoning tests with history content', *Archives de Psychologie*, 60, 225–42.

Smith, N. (1989) 'Geography as museum', in J. N. Entrikin and S. D. Brunn (eds) *Reflections on Richard Hartshorne's 'The Nature of Geography'* (Washington: Association of American Geographers).

Southworth, G. (1990) 'Leadership, headship and effective primary schools', *School Organisation*, 10(1), 3–16.

Steiner, M. (1989) 'Teaching and learning', in D. Hicks and M. Steiner, *op cit*.

Stenhouse, L. (1975) *An Introduction to Curriculum Research and Development* (London: Heinemann).

Sternberg, R. J. (1987) 'A day at developmental downs', *International Journal of Psychology*, 22, 507–29.

Stodolsky, S. (1988) *The Subject Matters* (Chicago: Chicago University Press).

Stoltman, J. P. (1991) 'Research on geography teaching', in J. P. Shaver, *op cit*.

Storm, M. (1970) 'Schools and the community', *Bulletin of Environmental Education*, 1.

Tann, S. (ed.) (1987) *Developing Topic Work in the Primary School*, (Lewes: The Falmer Press).

Thomas, A. (1992) 'Individualised teaching', *Oxford Review of Education*, 18(1), 59–74.

Thornton, S. J. (1988) *Critical Understandings of Curriculum in Practice: the case of social studies* (paper presented to AERA, New Orleans, La.).

Thornton, S. J. (1990) 'Should we be teaching more history?', *Theory and Research in Social Education*, 18(1), 53–60.

Thornton, S. J. (1991) 'Teacher as curricular-instructional gatekeeper in social studies', in J. P. Shaver, *op cit*.

Thornton, S. J. (1992) 'How do elementary teachers decide what to teach in social studies?', in E. W. Ross, J. W. Cornett and G. McCutcheon (eds) *Teacher Personal Theorizing: issues, problems and implications* (Albany, NY: State University of New York Press).

Thornton, S. and Vukelich, R. (1988) 'Effects of children's

understanding of time concepts on historical understanding', *Theory and Research in Social Education,* 16(1), 69–82.

Thornton, S. J. and Wenger, R. N. (1990) 'Geography curriculum and instruction in three fourth-grade classrooms', *The Elementary School Journal,* (90)5, 515–31.

Tosh, J. (1984) *The Pursuit of History* (London: Longman).

VanSickle, R. L. (1986) 'A quantitative review of research on instructional simulation gaming: a twenty year perspective', *Theory and Research in Social Education,* 14(3), 245–64.

Vygotsky, L. S. (1962) *Thought and Language* (Cambridge Ma: MIT Press).

Walford, R. (ed.) (1981) *Signposts for Geography Teaching* (London: Longman).

Walford, R. (1989) 'On the frontier with the new model army: geography publishing from the 1960s to the 1990s', *Geography,* 74(4), 308–20.

Walford, R. (1991) 'National curriculum: burden or opportunity?', *Teaching Geography,* 16(1), 32.

Walker, R. (1985) *Doing Research* (London: Routledge).

Walsh, W. H. (1967) *An Introduction to the Philosophy of History* (London: Hutchinson).

Weigand, P. (1991) 'The "known world" of primary school children', *Geography,* 76(1), 143–9.

Weigand, P. (1992) *Places in the Primary School* (Lewes: The Falmer Press).

Weinstein, C. S. (1990) 'Prospective elementary teachers' beliefs about teaching: implications for teacher education', *Teaching and Teacher Education,* 6(3), 279–90.

West, J. (1981) 'Children's awareness of the past' (Keele: unpublished PhD. thesis).

Wheldall, K. and Merrett, F. (1984) *Positive Teaching – the Behavioural Approach* (London: Allen and Unwin).

White, J. J. (1988) 'Searching for substantive knowledge in social studies texts', *Theory and Research in Social Education,* 16(2), 115–40.

Whitrow, G. J. (1988) *Time in History* (Oxford: Oxford University Press).

Wilen, W. W. and White, J. J. (1991) 'Interaction and discourse in social studies classrooms', in J. P. Shaver, *op cit.*

Williams, M. and Howley, R. (1989) 'Curriculum discontinuity: a study of a secondary school and its feeder primary schools', *British*

*Educational Research Journal,* 15(1), 61–76.

Wilson, B. L. and Corcoran, T. B. (1988) *Successful Secondary Schools* (Lewes: The Falmer Press).

Wilson, S. M. and Wineberg, S. S. (1988) 'Peering at history through different lenses', *Teachers' College Record,* 89(4), 525–39.

Wineberg, S. S. (1991) 'On the reading of historical texts', *American Educational Research Journal.*

Winitzky, N. (1992) 'Structure and process in thinking about classroom management', *Teaching and Teacher Education,* 18(1), 1–14.

Wittrock, M. C. (1986) 'Students' thought processes', in M. C. Wittrock, *op cit.*

Wittrock, M. C. (1986) *Handbook of Research on Teaching,* (New York: Macmillan).

Woff, R. (1991) 'The scope of the humanities', in P. Gordon, *op cit.*

Wragg, E. C., Bennett, S. N. and Carré, C. (1989) 'Primary teachers and the national curriculum', *Research Papers in Education,* 4(3), 17–45.

# Index

art
assessment 8, 53, 54, 63, 72, 91
attainment targets (ATs) 45, 62
citizenship 120, 121
common sense 2, 3, 22
concepts 21, 35, 59, 60, 68, 70, 72, 73, 94, 95, 108, 109, 116
co-operative learning – see *group-work*
cross-curricular themes 118–20
cultural differences 32–4
curriculum co-ordinators 6, 106, 107
direct instruction – see *recitations*
distant places 44, 52, 68–72
distant times 90, 95, 96
domain-specific understandings 26–8, 78, 104–6, 111
empathy – see *understanding others*
environmental education/studies 114, 115, 118, 119
European studies 44, 70, 104, 116–18
expertise 52, 67
feedback – see *assessment*
gender 10, 32–4, 66, 67, 74, 79, 99, 100
geography 38–82, 96, 102, 104
global education – see *world studies*
group-work 15, 17, 26, 33–5, 73–5, 98, 99
headteachers – see *leadership*
historical sources 83
historical time 67, 82, 92, 93
history 39, 58, 61, 64, 82–101, 103
implementation of innovations 7, 62, 107
individualisation 16
initial teacher education (ITE) 56
in-service education (INSET) – see *teacher development*
integration 39, 41, 42, 46, 48, 58, 84, 102–44
leadership 10, 11, 13
local studies 43, 50, 51, 59, 89–90, 113, 114–16
maps 42–5, 49, 50, 64–8, 116
materials – see *texts*

mathematics 18, 56, 59, 61, 63–5, 101, 109
metacognition 17, 35, 68, 77, 90, 97, 110
motivation 28–30, 35, 74, 75
National Curriculum (England) 43–5, 56, 62, 78, 86, 87, 100, 118
Piaget 25–7, 29, 30, 93, 95, 105
processes of enquiry 79, 115, 117
questioning 16, 20, 72, 73
reading 76, 77, 91, 96, 103
recitations 16, 17, 52–6, 61
research 1–5, 8, 9, 13, 14, 36, 49–50, 54, 57, 65–80, 89–100
resources – see *texts*
school effectiveness 6–13
science 31, 55, 63–5, 101
simulations and games 75
stereotypes 32, 35, 69–72
subject knowledge 18, 19, 47, 48, 56–8
teacher development 36, 57, 81, 100
teacher effectiveness 14–24, 36, 80
texts 59, 60, 63, 77, 91, 96, 97, 107
time for learning 60, 61, 111, 112
topic work – see *integration*
understanding others 33, 35, 48, 84, 85, 87, 93, 94
Vygotsky 26, 30, 32, 34, 73, 105
world studies 114–16, 119